LIGHT IN THE CITY

Learning faith in the city – in Hackney, East London.

Light in the City

Stories of the Church Urban Fund

by

MALCOLM GRUNDY

With a Foreword by

THE ARCHBISHOP OF CANTERBURY

The Canterbury Press
Norwich

British Library Cataloguing in Publication Data

Grundy, Malcolm
Light in the city: stories of the Church Urban Fund.
1. England. Urban regions. Inner areas. Society. Role of
Church of England
I. Title
261.10942

ISBN 1–85311–013–2

*Typeset by Rowland Phototypesetting Limited
Bury St Edmunds, Suffolk
and printed in Great Britain by
St Edmundsbury Press Limited, Suffolk*

Foreword

by His Grace The Archbishop of Canterbury

The publication of *Faith in the City* four years ago directed the attention of both Church and nation to the problems faced in our inner cities. It is sometimes forgotten that there were far more recommendations in the report which were addressed to the Church than to the nation as a whole.

The Church of England has taken those recommendations seriously and recognized its need to work in partnership with people in the inner cities, if there is to be renewal and the gifts of the people already there released. The Church Urban Fund is the most practical and public sign of the concern of the Church of England for the inner cities and the outer housing estates in our country.

Over two hundred projects have already been helped with their task of church and community building by the Church Urban Fund. Some of their stories are told in this book. It is an encouraging story and one which shows how the re-direction of resources enables people with imagination and flair to defeat hopelessness and restore self-confidence amongst those who too often feel powerless and rejected.

There is still work to be done. The Church of England has committed itself to raising eighteen million pounds in four years for the fund. The fund will enable the Church to support extra work in the inner cities for the next twenty years. I am glad that already we have this book to record the difference which such generosity targeted in the right places can bring.

Robert Cantuar

15th December 1989

*Photographs by Stefano Cagnoni (pp. 11, 15, 19, 23, 28, 33, 35, 37, 51, 57,
65, 77, 82, 85, 90, 98, 102, 115), John Applegate (pp. 49, 80, 112, 116, 121),
Paul Wilcox (p. 67), Paul Lowe (p. 88) and Daisy Hayes (frontispiece) are
used with permission.*
Cover design is by Sue Molineux

(*Acknowledgement*: the cartoon on page 4 appeared in the January 1986 issue of *Third Way*, and is reproduced by kind permission. *Third Way* seeks
to provide a biblical perspective on politics, social ethics and cultural affairs in the contemporary world. Further details and subscription rates: *Third
Way*, 2 Chester House, Pages Lane, London, N10 1PR.)
The cartoon on page 8 is reproduced by kind permission of MAC and Associated Newspapers plc.

Contents

Preface

There are many people in Britain who do not have a public or a political voice. Some are poor or lack the benefits of a good education, others have no home or no job. They are not organised into one of the groups who can exercise power in our society. In the descriptive chapters of this book I have tried to give them a voice. It has been a moving, exciting, sometimes depressing, but always a deeply spiritual experience to read through the submissions to the Church Urban Fund from applicants for grant aid.

The first two chapters and the last are entirely mine. The others are my piecing together of extracts, some short, some used or quoted at length, from grant applications. I have worked in this way so that those who have made submissions and those involved in the projects can have a voice. I must apologise to them if, with too much editing, I have misrepresented their situations.

I have always been made most welcome in the projects that I have visited but I could not have gone to all the 48 projects described here in the little over two months I had to produce the manuscript. Nor would it have been a good use of time and money since projects have been reported on in detail by sponsoring Dioceses and in many cases Urban Fund staff have also paid visits. Some of what is said in the descriptive chapters will be out of date since well over a year will have passed betweeen the writing of the application and the appearance of this book. I hope that the time gap will not weaken or discredit those strong urban voices.

My thanks go to Gordon Knights of The Canterbury Press Norwich for inviting me to write this book and to Kenneth Baker for seeing it through to publication. Jane Hustwit of the Church Urban Fund has supported and encouraged me through this and other pieces of work. All the projects mentioned here have been suggested by Jane and Geoff Marsh, the Fund's Projects Officers, and I am grateful to them for their wise guidance. Pat Healy has reported to The Fund on some projects and I have drawn on those reports for some of the descriptions and for some quotations from individuals. I am grateful to her for the use of these extracts.

To all those involved in work in urban areas I say, 'Keep up the applications. The Fund has a life of 20 years!' I hope that through the work of the Church Urban Fund it can be demonstrated that the Church has put its money where its heart should be. Concern for the voiceless, the poor and the disadvantaged must always be a central concern of our Christian gospel.

'Bear ye one another's burdens, and so fulfil the law of Christ.' (Galatians 6.2)

Advent 1989   MALCOLM GRUNDY

1

Finding Faith

'Conservative government leaks contents of controversial report to the press.' 'Government minister calls Church report a Marxist tract.' Newspaper headlines like these should come from the opening of a thriller or a novel by a modern Anthony Trollope. In real life they describe the events of the weekend of 1 November 1985.

Two years before those heady days, Robert Runcie, The Archbishop of Canterbury, announced that he was setting up a Commission. It would visit, research, and report to him about life in inner-city areas and their surrounding housing estates. A new catchphrase, Urban Priority Areas, came into use to describe these communities.

The Archbishop's concern for living conditions in these parts of England has been with him all his life. He grew up in Liverpool and knew much about the joys and pains of inner-city life. He also knew from his experience of Liverpool and many other cities about the vitality of the Christian faith of many people who live there. He knew about local churches struggling to keep afloat with old and difficult buildings. He had seen for himself in a city once torn by religious divisions what an inspiration and strength the Christian faith could be and, when roused, what a force church people are in trying to improve local conditions.

He has also always tried to listen to what those outside the churches are saying, so that it was no surprise in his enthronement sermon as Archbishop of Canterbury he said,

> 'I long to be able to speak while Archbishop with men and women who stand outside the Christian Church. I would like to say to them, "You can teach us so much if together we could look for the secret of the maze-like muddle in which the world finds itself." I ask for your prayers that I may be given the grace to speak like that and to listen . . .'

He was true to his word. In a series of visits during his first years as Archbishop he set out to see for himself what conditions were like, what the Churches were doing, and what they wanted to do, in urban areas.

These were also the years of much tension in cities across the country. Unemployment was high. Riots in Brixton had been followed by others in Bristol, Birmingham and Tottenham. Lord Scarman had produced his report, *The Brixton Disorders*, describing many of the problems of living in racially mixed areas and, in particular, difficulties in relations with the police. Visiting Brixton after the riots there, Robert Runcie promised action and greater understanding from the churches. Speaking about the presence of the churches in the inner-city, he told the Birmingham Community Relations Council in July 1982:

'There are, of course, temptations to withdraw from the inner-cities. The work is costly and difficult. There is often little response. In some areas we have had to close churches and to withdraw workers but, as far as I have any influence, I am determined that we should maintain our presence in the most sensitive areas and allocate our resources accordingly.'

So, on 6 July 1983 the Archbishop called a press conference to announce the setting up of his Commission. It was to be chaired by Sir Richard O'Brien, who until recently had been Chairman of the Manpower Services Commission. Also to be members were The Rt Revd David Sheppard, Bishop of Liverpool and The Rt Revd Wilfred Wood, Bishop of Croydon, the first black Anglican Bishop in England.

There were clergy and lay people with experience of inner-city areas. The Trades Unions were represented by Ron Keating, Assistant General Secretary of the National Union of Public Employees, and industrialists by David Booth, Executive Director of B.I.C.C. There were academics and a theologian, Anthony Harvey, Canon of Westminster Abbey. In this Church of England venture there were also people from other denominations and a particularly significant contribution was made by Robina Rafferty from the Catholic Housing Aid Society.

The Commission took two years to collect its evidence and visited 41 cities and estates across England. Because they discovered a lively faith in many of the places they visited, the commissioners gave their report the title *Faith in the City*. It was this report which caused such a stir in government circles and its recommendations which prompted the pre-publication 'leak' to the press.

The Times carried as its main headline on Monday 2 December:

'Church and State launched into new public quarrel – "Marxist" slur on inner-city report.'

As well as the leak to the press an unattributed government minister had called the report 'Marxist'. Such a swift reaction, far from stealing a march on the publication of the report, was regarded by many as an 'own goal' by the government which drew more public attention to the report than would otherwise have been likely. Many of those who would never dream of reading a 'religious' book or of going into a Christian bookshop found themselves beating a path to the doors in a rush to purchase their copies.

Other press reaction was swift with those on the political right joining forces in condemnation. Paul Johnson, writing in the *Daily Mail* the next day called it 'a flawed gospel that is beneath contempt'. He thought the report was part of a take-over by left-wing activists who were infiltrating our national institutions. In a classic piece of popular journalism he wrote,

'Like other institutions in rapid decline, it (the Church of England) is an easy target for take-over by Left-Wing activists. This is what has been happening in recent years. The present document is a typical consequence.

It is a new kind of curate's egg – bad all through, but with some parts worse than others. Now that the whole text is available, it is clear that it is not, as one Cabinet Minister has claimed, a Marxist document.

It has no such coherence. It varies from hand-flapping waffle to the cliché-ideology of the Polytechnocracy, with a few nuggets of Bennery thrown in. Intellectually it is beyond contempt.'

There was more of the same kind of criticism in other newspapers, some of it very obviously from people who had not read the report.

At the other end of the political spectrum, Frank Field, writing in *The Guardian* condemned the report for being too mild in its recommendations. With others, he suggested that it was lacking in any vision of Christian justice. In an article on 8 December, he wrote,

'. . . the Commission did not address itself to the right questions . . . While the report is a first-class piece of work . . . it could have been produced by any group of decent minded individuals. What should have made it special and different from secular efforts was its theology – of God's vision of the world, the nature of man and his part in working out this design. Instead of this being the starting point, the theological analysis is tacked on to the end. Typically the report begins not with a reference to scripture but to a Government White Paper.'

The general public reception of the report was that the evidence it contained was indeed disturbing. While many disagreed with the recommendations, few could argue against the need for urgent action. Attempts were made to estimate the cost of implementing the report's proposals, a task not done in the report. A general view was that they might require as much a rise in the standard rate of Income Tax of 4p in the pound.

Third Way, January 1986

Let the last word from the press following the launch of *Faith in the City* come in a Private-Eye send-up by Lombard in the *Financial Times* of 5 December:

'A government minister last night described as "Communist filth" the cover of a forthcoming Institute of Directors report of an inquiry into manufacturing industry entitled, "Could we possibly do a little better?"

The Minister said the title "betrayed its Marxist envy of other nations and the quite explicit extreme left-wing desire to impose equality on everybody through the lash and the jack-boot."

He said he had not read the report and did not intend to: but that "a glance at the title page was quite enough for me, thank you very much." A copy of the report, to be published soon, is in the hands of the *Financial Times*. It lashes out savagely at the government for "perhaps on occasion being a little harsh on some of the less efficient of our industries in pursuit of the wholly laudable aim of competitiveness and higher profitability."

A senior Cabinet minister, to whom this passage was read, commented that "The Institute of Directors has been hopelessly infiltrated by Trotskyists mouthing this kind of garbage. It is rank socialism, a thinly disguised ambition to subsidise a plethora of dying industries in order to suborn their employees and turn them into a private army of red thugs".'

The whole event of the leak and of the publication of *Faith in the City* gave the press a field day. It also showed what confusion can be caused within the ranks of the establishment, let alone with the public, when a national institution like the Church of England publishes a report which brings into the open the problems of a particular section of English society who do not have a voice of their own – except on occasion to riot in the streets.

So, after all the smokescreen and excitement of the launch, what did *Faith in the City* actually say? Certainly its 398 pages are no easy read. The great strength of the report is its argument from factual, statistical evidence, much of it gathered from actual government documents. Each chapter begins with a quotation from a person in an area visited by the Commissioners; for example we have:

'It is difficult to avoid the conclusion that one is living in an area that is being . . . treated with hostility by the rest of society.' (*Vicar in Greater Manchester*)

'We're far too busy to have a strategy.' (*Vicar to new curate in East London*)

'To someone who has had electricity cut off because they cannot pay a bill of £70, it may seem scandalous that churches spend hundreds on perhaps unnecessary improvements to church buildings and furnishings.' (*Advice worker in London*)

'It is not charity when the powerful help the poor . . . it is justice.' (*Diocese of Liverpool*)

'Behind the statistics are real people, like the 50 year old man who cried when offered a place on a M.S.C. scheme because he felt wanted again.' (*Black Country Urban Industrial Mission*)

But in the chapters themselves the emphasis is on facts and figures. There are few examples of life and work in Urban Priority Areas. What this careful statistical analysis did do was to establish the extent of the problem.

From the 1981 Census the Department of the Environment was able to describe characteristics of urban areas which would show a certain kind of deprivation. They are:

- ★ A high level of unemployment
- ★ Many old people living alone
- ★ Single-parent families
- ★ A mix of people from several ethnic backgrounds
- ★ Overcrowded homes
- ★ Homes lacking basic amenities

A so called U.P.A. will have some or all of these characteristics. They can be measured and when these calculations are added together, they produce what rather unattractively are called 'Z scores'. These will be referred to again in chapter two when we look at how decisions are made about placing resources in U.P.A.s.

The report itself is divided into three sections. The first part is descriptive – the story of economic decline, the run-down of some of our major industries, poor housing and physical and social decay in U.P.A.s is told. Then the present work of the church in these areas is described with strong memories of previous attempts at work in inner-city parishes.

In Part Two, the report looks at the question what kind of church will be needed to work in these areas in the future. Many questions are posed. What is the most effective way to deploy people and money? Can the urban church ever be truly local, not always staffed and supported by outsiders? What is the different nature of the problems here? Do the clergy and lay workers need special training? What can be done to adapt or re-use inappropriate buildings? How best can lay people be supported and equipped? Is it possible for the comparative wealth of suburban and rural dioceses to be channelled towards areas of need? In this section there was also the seed idea that a Church Urban Fund should be set up so that financial resources could be targeted to specifically designated areas.

Prophetically, the report suggests certain characteristics which should be striven for in U.P.A. parishes. What kind of a church would grow and thrive naturally? The report is fairly strong in its opinions. A church which is made up of local people, reflecting the mix of those who live there. A church committed to working in its own area and with other local community groups. A church which is outward-looking, which sees as part of its mission an active servant role in the life of the neighbourhood. A church which sees God at work in the whole of society and not only among its members. A church which is participative, able to listen to the needs of all its members and able to develop a collaborative method of working between clergy and lay people. A participative church will also want to work alongside those of other denominations and, where appropriate, establish Local Ecumenical Projects to give formal recognition to co-operation and common mission in an area.

Nothing would be more delightful than for these characteristics to be seen in all our churches. It is a great tribute to the spiritual vitality of many U.P.A. parishes and to the leadership of their Bishops and clergy that such characteristics might especially be thought possible here. If successful, even in part, what a gift these so-called impoverished areas would have to give to the rest of the church. They would show us all that riches and poverty can be seen in many different ways.

It was the report's third section of recommendations to the nation which drew most attention and which, as we have seen, aroused much public controversy. Many of the recommendations were about central government policy and called for greater public spending. (See Appendix I)

With the hindsight of a few years many of the recommendations seem dated. We know that other solutions have been attempted, particularly those favoured by a Conservative government through the 1980s which encourage private capital into these areas. An extreme criticism of *Faith in the City* is that it was recommending Sixties solutions to the problems of a world which had moved on.

'For years the Church laboured on this report brethren, but does anyone listen?'

However, the publicity which surrounded the report drew public attention to the problems of the inner-city. *Faith in the City* and the Scarman Report about the riots in Brixton are two of the publicly recognised documents which spell out all the difficulties of racism, housing and family life, poverty, unemployment, and tensions with the police which were real life for inner-city and housing estate dwellers in the 1980s. They have become important social benchmarks which will be referred to as a measure of our corporate life by generations to come.

'What did you do in the war Daddy?' will now be superseded by many with the questions to themselves, and to Church and Nation alike, 'What did you do about *Faith in the City*?' What the Church of England, with the other denominations, did and is doing, is a remarkable tale of giving and action.

2

Funding Faith

It is one of the miracles of this century that the publication of *Faith in the City* was able to push such a conservative and bureaucratic Church into action so quickly. The first public move was the appointment of an Archbishop's Officer for Urban Priority Areas, the Reverend, now Prebendary, Patrick Dearnley.

To back up the work of Pat Dearnley, the Rt Revd Tom Butler, Bishop of Willesden, was asked to chair a support group. It soon became clear that very little thought had been given by the Commission to the way in which their proposals would be followed up. Bishop Butler also discovered that few financial resources had been set aside for Pat to do his work or for adequate support to be given. Much banging on the gates of Lambeth Palace had to be done before the flagship of A.C.U.P.A. could set out from port. The support group soon became an Advisory Group, working with Pat on pressing for the implementation of at least some of the A.C.U.P.A. proposals and monitoring the progress of others.

There had to be a twofold strategy. The proposals for change made to the Church and to the nation had to be pressed at senior level, with government ministers and through the church's parliament, the General Synod. At the same time a network of local contacts had to be established across the country. Each Diocese was asked to appoint a link officer to promote debate about the report and the implementation of its proposals in their areas. These link officers are vital, applying the general findings of A.C.U.P.A. to their local churches, whether they are urban, suburban or rural.

The report gave urban parishes one thing in particular to get their teeth into. At the end of the book there was the suggestion that local churches should carry out a survey or audit to discover exactly what conditions were like in their own area. An audit contains social analysis – facts and figures about unemployment and employment, housing, family life, ethnic groups, church life and the like, followed by a plan for action developed from the information discovered. Very many parishes used a form of this audit, or one designed locally. This work, valuable in itself, also demonstrated whether or not a parish was in an Urban Priority Area. Their Z scores told all, so a row of railway cottages in an otherwise affluent area would not qualify.

The Church Urban Fund

The Fund's establishment evolved directly from *Faith in the City* – one of its many major recommendations. Building on the work of the Church in the inner city areas and the outer estates, the Fund supports the development of practical projects in urban priority areas, enabling local people to meet their spiritual, social and economic needs.

The recommendation to establish the Fund was put to the General Synod in February 1986. By June 1987 the Church Urban Fund was set up as a company limited by guarantee and had been registered as a charity; trustees had been appointed and an operational structure devised.

The Church Urban Fund
- is for those in our cities who are poor, disadvantaged and feel excluded from the mainstream of our national and Church life;
- assists work that addresses the fundamental issues raised in *Faith in the City*;
- is a practical demonstration that the Church as a whole is concerned for and stands with the deprived;
- aims to help the people of deprived urban communities find and implement ways of meeting the spiritual and material needs of their own communities. It helps *locally* based projects and initiatives;
- works in two ways – it makes grants for projects from its own resources; and it provides a vehicle for sponsorship by corporate and Trust donors.

The Trustees favour applications for projects which:
- build on the existing presence of the Church;
- demonstrate ecumenical working;
- are clearly managed by and/or employ members of the local community.

A project may specifically promote the Christian message or may more generally address community needs.

Both innovatory and proven ideas will be supported.

The Fund was launched with a grand service of dedication in Westminster Abbey on 20 April 1988. A new national charity was born, created specifically to work with those suffering from poverty and to bring light into the inner-cities of England. H.M. The Queen is patron of the Fund, which is chaired by the Archbishop of Canterbury.

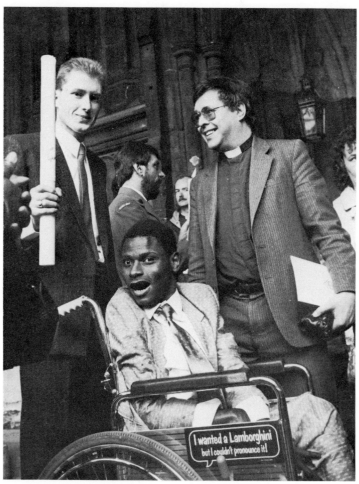

The Birmingham delegation at the launch of the Church Urban Fund, Westminster Abbey, April 1988.

Every diocese was represented at this service. The centrepiece of which was the lighting of 43 large candles, one for each diocese. These were then taken by their bearers down the Abbey, through the great West doors and out into the spring sunshine and the streets of Westminster. Bearers were then asked to take these candles, symbolic of light in dark places, back to their home dioceses.

Now the task of fund raising had begun in earnest. The Fund was charged with raising enough so that £4 million could be spent on projects each year. It was calculated that this would require a capital sum of £18 million bearing in mind that the Fund was intended to spend itself out of existence by about 2010. At this time it was felt that the £18 million would take between two and four years to raise – from the dioceses of the Church of England.

Fund raising is a highly competitive and sophisticated activity. The working party responsible for creating the Church Urban Fund recognised this and employed an experienced team of professional fund raisers, based at Lambeth Palace, as well as a fund raising consultant. Detailed advice had shown that the campaign should be organised on a diocesan basis. It was also equally clear that effective fund raising activities need to be structured – with targets. So the total of £18 million was divided between the 43 dioceses, asking most from those parts of the country where prosperity is greatest and church life strongest. Each diocese eventually accepted their target and set up a more or less sophisticated fund raising operation.

The dioceses have tackled their commitment to support the Church Urban Fund in a wide variety of ways. The energy and enthusiasm has been remarkable, particularly when there have been so many other financial demands facing churches everywhere – some dioceses have unilaterally increased their own targets. The more successful dioceses have all followed a similar strategy – strong leadership, the setting of targets at deanery or parish level, the provision of regular feedback on the achievement of these targets and the undertaking of a programme of fund raising events which have included always some initiatives with very steep targets. On the day these have usually been achieved or surpassed.

Good organisation and hard work, supporting a well thought out structure, have meant that the Church Urban Fund is well on the way to the £18 million. However it is the stunts and special events that always catch the eye. Here the eccentricities of the Church of England come into their own.

The Reverend Donald Brockbank and his wife were among those taking part in a 'sponsored abscond' from Birkenhead. The participants were given 12 hours to get as far away as they could. Five hand-cuffed pairs set out wearing white 'convict' jackets with arrows on. Between them the couples clocked up 1,500 miles. Mr and Mrs Brockbank got to John O'Groats, while other couples reached Edinburgh, Luton and Plymouth and back in the allotted time.

At St Bartholomew's, Yealmpton, Exeter, two members of the P.C.C. parachuted 2,500 feet after only a day's training. They raised £1,000 of the parish's £1,300 target.

A cheque arrived at Lambeth from a parishioner at St Paul's, Mill Hill, who had been collecting and selling manure!

Other events have been more ambitious. A successful fund raising event in the early days of the Fund was an auction at Gorhambury House (St Albans Diocese). There were 240 lots which raised £19,500. The auction was conducted by the chairman of Phillips Fine Arts Auctioneers. A concert in Gloucester Cathedral in August 1988 raised £21,000. It featured famous soloists, Martyn Hall (tenor) and Lucy Wakeford (harp) with the National Youth Chamber Orchestra.

The London Diocese used the parable of the talents to raise money for the Fund. At a service in St Paul's Cathedral in 1988 parishes collected £100 each. They used this seed money to raise as much as possible in the space of a year. The success of the venture was celebrated in St Paul's at Pentecost 1989 by which time parishes had sent in £318,000.

The most ubiquitous of all the fund raisers were the Vardy family. They spent the summer of 1989 busking around the cathedrals of England. Dr Peter Vardy, his wife Anne and their children Christian, Luke, Catherine, Leah and Kirsten covered over 700 miles and visited 20 cathedrals, raising the public profile of the Fund everywhere they went.

The highlight of the fund raising campaign in 1989 was Church Urban Fund week, 17–24 September. Supporting the theme of 'Light in the City', thousands of little red candles were sold to raise money for the Fund and services of dedication to the Fund were held all over the country, alongside fund raising events. The week culminated with a service in Coventry Cathedral, led by the Archbishop of Canterbury and was supported throughout, in the true spirit of British public broadcasting by coverage on B.B.C. Radio 4's *The Archers*.

Busking for the Church Urban Fund:
the Vardy family, Summer 1989

Music and drama have played an important part in supporting fund raising and raising social issues. The Jabbok theatre company from Leeds was commissioned by the Fund to write and present a contemporary parable. It is the story of Lazarus and Dives, the same story which inspired Albert Schweitzer to go to Lambarene. The play, called 'Up the Wall', is set at the scene of the Last Judgement. Laz Harris is placed with the sheep. D. Ives is placed with the goats. But why? Has Ives not treated Laz as he should have done? Did he see the inner-city where Laz lived and then pass him by on the other side? A wall is placed between them. The play asks the question, can the Church Urban Fund and ordinary Christians do anything about removing the wall which divides rich and poor in England?

Not all the finance for the Fund is derived from the diocesan contributions.

Financial support for the Church Urban Fund is also being made available from elsewhere. The Church Commissioners are providing the Fund with £1 million each year as well as supplying generous support through staff secondments and administrative help.

The actress and the Bishop launching Church Urban Fund week, September 1989: Ellie Darvill and the Bishop of Warwick preparing to take off in a hot air balloon in the grounds of Warwick castle.

Although the main fundraising activity, as a matter of policy, has been expected from the parishes, industry, commerce and the financial sector are playing their part.

A few eminent Christian businessmen were consulted in the early stages of the Fund's formation, and agreed that there was scope for the involvement of the corporate organisations in the work of the Church Urban Fund. There are certain aspects of this work which they find particularly relevant, such as training and employment initiatives. But the range of projects directly sponsored by companies perhaps indicates that 'self-interest' is not the over-ruling motivation. There is a growing desire on the part of companies to become more involved with their local communities, and the churches (in the shape of the Church Urban Fund) can provide the means for them to do this.

Many companies have given cash with no strings attached, with contributions up to £200,000, others prefer a closer link. For instance, B.P. and the National Westminster Bank have directed their money towards specific projects including work with the homeless in Hull and a community business enterprise in Sheffield. British Gas, Lloyds Bank and the Midland Bank have given help to specific projects where they can involve their personnel in practical ways, such as part-time professional help and training.

Barclays Bank, Whitbreads and Prudential are making their main contribution through secondment. Allied Lyons have also seconded an employee as Diocesan Business Adviser to four Northern Dioceses jointly. I.B.M. is involving its personnel in community work on a part-time basis to projects in Manchester. I.C.I. are giving support where they have local operations, enabling their regional managers to consult locally on the most effective way of involving staff.

Eagle Star has agreed to support an imaginative youth project in Birmingham. Northern Rock is sponsoring a community centre in Newcastle. Tyne-Tees Television is spreading its support over a variety of projects in the North East. John Laing has chosen to link with a project for the elderly in Middlesbrough. The Post Office has helped with cash, equipment and vehicles. I.C.L. has offered computer equipment for training programmes and Legal and General has provided a van. Hammerson (Developers) are sponsoring a project for the homeless in Wolverhampton.

Many dioceses have also approached local trusts and companies to boost local appeals and projects, and are building up longer-term links.

Let the last word on fund-raising come from a letter sent to Jane Hustwit, the Church Urban Fund's Communications Director:

> The most regular givers in the Winchester Diocese are twin sisters aged 83. They have sent donations on five separate occasions and the only problem they pose is how I can say thank you nicely, and differently, on each occasion. I have just heard from one of the ladies

who has thanked me for my two most recent letters together with a copy of the C.U.F. News and the Diocesan insert. I cannot think of a truer example of real Christian giving than shown by these two ladies. I quote selectively from this most recent letter:

'We cannot do much in a practical way for the church but when we draw our pensions each week we can set aside a little for the Church Urban Fund. My sister worked for nearly 40 years as a nurse at Guy's Hospital and later as Matron of King's College Hospital. Whilst with Guy's she helped to nurse some of the men wounded at Dunkirk. I qualified as a psychiatric social worker at the London School of Economics in the 1930s and then worked in the London Juvenile Courts in Toynbee Hall and Southwark before there was any welfare state. When the war came and the children were sent out of London we went after them to try and help with their distress. My chief concern will always be for young deprived children and adolescents from all social classes. From a school run by the Society of St Francis I learned this prayer: "O Father of the forsaken and Lover of the unloved, make us bearers of Your Presence to all." '

The good lady asked that no reply need be sent, but we have had the splendid idea of going down to where they live to take them out to lunch. I don't think you will see it as a Diocesan expense!

3

Families and Children

Bad housing, low incomes and unemployment have an inescapable effect on a community. Inescapable is the most appropriate word. Pressure on family life is great, often beyond breaking point. Single parent families, marriage breakdown, alcoholism, vandalism and drug taking are the bitter consequences. With applications to finance projects, the Fund's Trustees have been given dramatic accounts of life in these communities. Here are powerful, typical, examples.

St Cuthbert's, Gateshead

St Cuthbert's is a severely deprived parish in the North Bensham and Low Teams area of Gateshead. Most of the original industry has gone. The community suffers from unemployment (26 per cent), crime, vandalism and long-term decay.

The Church Urban Fund was asked to support the employment of a Pastoral Assistant, Terry Dawson, to work alongside the local vicar to develop community activities, especially among families and local children. A grant of £21,210 has been made. It will be spread over three years.

There is obvious poverty in the parish. The housing is in need of repair and there is graffiti everywhere including the initials LTAG – Low Teams Aggro Group. Yet here is a living community. It has already been physically torn in two by a large dual carriageway built right through the middle. The road was imposed on the community, and the subway which links the two sides has provided ample extra space for the graffiti artists.

Terry has now become an established person in the area, developing the professional skills he needs to do his job. He works closely with Sr Bernadette, a Roman Catholic nun and community worker, who decided to live among the local people and on whose behalf she feels intense anger.

Sr Bernadette says the project began when a local G.P. called everyone together because she wanted to do something about growing apathy and depression; the churches have now come in on an ecumenical basis.

The Revd John Parker, vicar of St Cuthbert with St Paul who chairs the management committee, says that the needs of the area came to his notice through the support group, started in response to the G.P.'s initiative. The Church of England had 'a very weak response to need' and then it was thought that the Fund might pay the salary of a worker 'to sustain what we already do in the parish, rather than bring an outsider into the situation.'

The G.P., Dr Margaret Sherratt, says the support group began because a health visitor thought it would be a good idea for everybody to get together. Dr Sheratt was seeing people with tension and headaches caused by social problems.

Children at the local primary school are a top priority for Terry Dawson, worker at St Cuthbert's, Bensham.

She says it was 'daft to be working alone rather than getting together' to support each other. All the professionals were doing demanding jobs dealing with just one part of the same problem. She says the idea snowballed. The support group began with three mothers – not just another toddler group, but specially created to build up their confidence.

One of their ideas was to get the Manpower Services Commission to fund a worker to visit lonely old people. That idea was successful, and Terry Dawson worked for one year as a 'befriender' with 'Christian Relay'. Now the Urban Fund grant enables him to remain in the area and continue his work. A lot of people sit at home alone and don't get out: Terry encourages them to go out to the centre for coffee mornings, old time dancing and many other activities.

Dr Sherratt finds comments by some politicians unhelpful: 'you can't afford to make your own soup every day, when you can't get money because you are unemployed. It is pointless to expect people to stop smoking when there is evidence, including a B.M.A. report, equating stress with unemployment, poor housing and low wages. You can't blame people for smoking when there is so much stress. You need to relieve the causes of stress' she says.

It does depress her that people don't take preventative care, but she points to some of the reasons. The Townsend survey, *Inner city deprivation and premature death (1988)*, found that about 100 wards locally were worse than Tower Hamlets, with the death rate in Bensham nearly twice as high as the average. St Cuthbert's Church has at least 100 funerals a year.

Dr Sherratt is encouraged that the project is beginning to have an impact on people's lives. Mothers are more confident and elderly people get out more. Terry's role, linking church, the community and local organisations, is crucial in this.

His working week includes helping out at the local primary and nursery schools – a favourite task is driving infants to a local leisure centre where they have a great time on the inflatables in the 'soft play area'. There are also church visits, counselling the bereaved, preparing baptisms – and organising the Team community festival which has been going for the past two years.

Terry says the festival includes a beer tent 'to get the fathers involved', a five-a-side football team, bands, dancing, a fun run which gets families involved and a pub quiz. Sr Bernadette commented 'it was great seeing the clergy and nuns all drinking together in the pub like they were part of the community'.

Northam, Southampton

Acute concern was expressed by the local head teacher, health visitors, school governors and the local church, about the welfare of children and young people in Northam. The Church Urban Fund is financing a part-time community social worker to help parents with very young children to understand their own and their children's needs and to encourage them to meet these needs from their own resources as well as from those provided by statutory and voluntary organisations. The Fund has awarded a grant of £18,000 to be spent over three years.

Northam lies in the centre of Southampton and is part of the parish of Southampton City Centre, which is a U.P.A. It is bounded by the main London to Southampton railway line, the River Itchen and industrial development bordering the now rarely used docks railway line. It is bisected by the main easterly road into Southampton over the River Itchen. The population of around 1500, is housed either in 24 blocks of 1960s three-storey Council flats, with one 15-storey point block, or in pre-1914 houses. There is a small parade of shops, not all of which are used for retail purposes, and a First School with 60 children and a further 40 Nursery School places. The School population has roughly one third ethnic minority children.

There is little play space and what there is is tarmac-surfaced with small amounts of Council-provided equipment. The only public grassed area in Northam is on the opposite side of the major easterly trunk road from the Council flats and though the Northam estate has grassed areas, ball games are prohibited.

The 1981 Census statistics show that in the area unemployment was around 20 per cent, the average for Southampton being 9 per cent and car ownership was under 30 per cent. For the parish as a whole, in July 1987 unemployment was at the level of 26 per cent: 1988, the 0–5 child population was 200 in Northam.

The Project arises out of acute concern expressed by the local Head Teacher, Health Visitors, School Governors and the local church, for young children in Northam. The Head Teacher reports that an unusually high number of children are entering the Nursery School, in the area, with delayed development. Of the children, at present in the Nursery and likely to enter the First School in Northam by 1990, 26 per cent do not speak English at home; 28 per cent have medical problems (hearing and vision defects); 28 per cent exhibit developmental delays; 35 per cent have behavioral problems; 46 per cent have social or emotional problems and 54 per cent have communication difficulties; over 40 per cent have three or more of these. Nearly half the children entering the First School, from the Nursery in 1989, have some sort of behavioral problems. In this area, numbers of families are moving into the area from Bed and Breakfast accommodation and this trend is likely to increase.

This state of affairs in the Nursery School gives staff and Governors concern as the children cause serious problems for the staff within the Nursery. This has serious implications for the children themselves as they enter the First School with some handicap which will almost certainly place them at a disadvantage, as well as creating management problems for the school.

Social workers, working in the area, find that in Northam their caseload among families with children is 73 per cent above normal for the central area of Southampton, which again gives rise to concern.

Further, in a survey commissioned by the Parish of Southampton City Centre and carried out in 1986, 'Women and Children in St Mary's and Nicholstown', a nearby area, some of the difficulties and attitudes which affect the mothers in the area were highlighted, and proposals for further work suggested. In general, the mothers were resentful of the attitudes of outsiders and of the statutory agencies. Some spoke poignantly of the problems facing them as parents in bringing up children in the area. The report suggested the employment of community workers in the area.

Money from the Church Urban Fund has helped to appoint such a community worker who will co-operate with other local agencies in Northam. The work is with individual parents and with groups of parents, especially those who feel isolated or vulnerable. The emphasis is on helping them to develop confidence in themselves so that mutual support can grow. It is hoped that in this way some of the self-identified problems in this community can be tackled by the residents themselves. In the long-term it will be their children who will gain.

St Augustine's, Halifax

St Augustine's parish is on the north western side of Halifax town centre, to the east of Queen's Road. It has a population of approximately two thousand. Originally an area of terraced working class housing, it now has the predominantly Pakistani population characteristic of this area of Halifax. Most of the immigrants arrived in the 1950s from a poor rural area where their villages were to be flooded to form a reservoir. Most are Sunni (moderate) Muslims, although the occasional Sikh can be seen. The local councillor is a Muslim, representing the Labour Party, but it is symptomatic of the stresses on the Pakistani family caused by the changing pattern of life, that his wife and children have returned permanently to Pakistan. Women are beginning to feel downtrodden as the barriers disappear, but their husbands prevent them from learning English and from going out to work. As the Pakistanis become more affluent, they are beginning to leave the area to move into larger houses, and are being replaced by single-parent families. The other chief component of the population are the elderly, many of whom live in sheltered accommodation where they are almost trapped, being afraid to go out at night.

St Augustine's parish does not have a church. The building was demolished in 1972 after many of the local congregation had moved away. There were such low attendances that the church was closed down as a place of worship.

Since then, St Augustine's Centre has become a focus for the community. It consists of the church school, a community park, a modern vicarage and St Augustine's House, the former Victorian vicarage now converted into a centre to serve the local community. There is also the 'Good News' charity shop, which sells second-hand clothes and bric-a-brac at rock bottom prices. The Church Urban Fund has contributed £10,000 towards the establishment of St Augustine's House. Since the church was demolished, services have been held in the school hall – now named the Prayer Hall, an idea picked up in India by the vicar, the Revd John Bunker. The new chapel in St Augustine's House, like much of the rest of the conversion, was designed by the vicar, an architect before he became a priest. It is elegant and simple with bench seating around the walls and space to bring in chairs for congregations of more than twenty.

The area where the church used to stand is now the community park area, with the foundation stones of the church incorporated into the design. The park is used for open air services, theatres and fêtes – and by local people as a restful meeting place. The park contains a memorial tree to Edith Nettleton, a parish missionary who was martyred in China in 1931.

The lack of an actual church building is one of the things that

John Bunker visits a local shop in Halifax.

gives the project great potential in John Bunker's view. The second factor is that 'in 1981 the Church said they needed a Christian presence in the area', despite the apparently unpromising prospects. He says that somehow £93,000 has been raised for the project over two years.

Alongside major grants, one local source of income is the church's charity shop, officially called the 'Good News' shop but known locally as the 'Good as New' shop. It is situated between the elderly and Muslim areas and forms a lively frontier of meeting between the various elements of the community. It was opened in 1979 and was purchased by the church in 1985 at a cost of £7,000. In 1986 it had an income of almost £2,000 from sales in the shop and the rent of the flat above it. The shop is staffed by volunteers from the congregation who find it a very enjoyable and worthwhile form of service in the life of the parish and the community.

John Bunker says about his place in the community: 'I don't believe I am a social worker. I am a priest of the church. The church said a Christian presence should be here, and you have to have a priest to look after that.'

'Our kind of church is the only institution which exists for the faith of the outsider,' he says. 'I think the church exists for the benefit of those outside. In other words, we want the church to serve the neighbourhood with no strings attached.'

The church school reflects the neighbourhood: seventy per cent Asian on a school roll of nearly 200. Ten years ago there were ten Asians in the school. Some of the other schools in the area have no white children.

Despite the predominance of Asian children, school assembly is clearly Christian – they use the B.B.C. schools hymn book *Love and Praise*. The Asian children know the words and music as well as the whites. The vicar and John Fleming, the headmaster, both say that local Asians send their children to the school because they approve of the moral atmosphere.

Fleming, who was born in Halifax, found the area completely changed when he returned in 1968 from a three-year stint teaching in Finchley. When he left there were 6 Asian children in a school population of 245. There is only one Asian teacher in the four local primary schools.

Like Mrs Bunker, who is an English teacher at a nearby school, Fleming is concerned that separate language classes provided by Calderdale L.E.A. were recently found to be 'racist' resulting in the classes and children being integrated into the normal school.

Fleming says that the theory is that children pick up language naturally, which is fine in theory. The weakness lies in the fact that there are not many white children at the school for them to pick it up from. He agrees there are English classes for adults and concedes 'it is bound to be overcome in time – it is less severe than it was'. But there is still resistance in Asian homes to allow mothers out for language classes. Language classes are now provided by the local authority and take place in St Augustine's House. Fleming says that there have been cases where the last remaining white family in a street have 'felt very threatened' although they have no reason to, but says that the community by and large has been very harmonious.

The school invites elderly people in for coffee mornings. The existence of an 'old folks ghetto' next to an Asian one makes the former very fearful of the Asians. But that is changing: one lady works regularly in the school and at home helps the Asian adults a lot. She came as a lonely old pensioner and goes into their homes where she is welcome. This part of the church is a mission front.

The headmaster says that John Bunker, who takes one assembly a week, has an ability to relate to everyone easily: 'He is pioneering a way, a pattern, for churches of the future. He is breaking down barriers and making churches more relevant to the needs of the community.' The passing of the traditional church 'makes Christianity more relevant to this day and age,' he says.

Mrs Shammi Malik, multi-cultural liaison officer for Calderdale Health Authority, confirms some of the needs the church is meeting. She has worked in the area for 17 years, speaks six languages and is greeted in several of them.

Pakistani youths harass both elderly whites and non-Pakistani Asians. Shammi says she tries to get the parents to do something but they have largely given up. The AIDS scare means that Asian men will no longer use English girls as prostitutes – so they are sending Asian schoolgirls over to Leeds or Bradford. Inter-racial rivalry between Asian groups precludes outside help: Shammi knows of more than one project that could have attracted E.E.C. Social Fund money being lost because the leaders would not agree that projects should be open to all nationalities.

The Church Urban Fund's specific contribution has been towards the conversion of the large black Yorkshire stone former vicarage into the St Augustine's Centre. Downstairs, as well as the chapel, it houses comfortable rooms where Asian women can learn English. Upstairs must seem like Heaven on Earth to many parents. There is a large, well equipped playroom; a kitchen where cookery, diet and budgeting can be learned. There is a toy library where toys and books can be borrowed and a rest room where exhausted mothers, or fathers, can sleep for an hour while their children play. St Augustine's, Halifax is a remarkable example of what can be done with energy, dedication and vision.

Maryport, Carlisle

When the Hillside Estate in the seaside town of Maryport, Cumbria, was built in 1972 it won design awards for its red-bricked flat roofed maisonettes. Now many are boarded up after being vandalised and the local council is considering whether it should give up and sell the whole estate off.

The problems for the residents were clear from the start. What may have looked like model homes on paper, proved to be disastrous to live in because of the flat roofs, poor insulation, inadequate heating and condensation. It is deeply depressing for the families still living there, surrounded by boarded up blocks and deliberately shattered low brick walls, and remote from most forms of transport.

'But they have been promised so much and given so little, that they don't believe things can ever get better,' says the Revd Noel Carter, vicar of All Souls' Church, Netherton.

The report inspired the Revd Mike Diggle, diocesan officer of the Carlisle Board for Social Responsibility, to start discussions with the Anglican, Catholic and Methodist Churches and the local authority to consider what might be done.

They concluded that the area desperately needed a community worker, although they knew previous attempts had proved disastrous when the wrong person was appointed. The estate's only community 'building' apart from the Church was a now abandoned and boarded up portakabin.

But their concern was sufficiently strong and persuasive that it is now beginning to happen. A £60,000 community centre is being built, financed mainly by a local housing association with additional grants from the local council and the M.S.C. The community worker has been appointed with the salary met by the Church Urban Fund.

All who work in the community have to deal with both apathy and hostility from the local people. 'Offsiders' – unless they wear clerical collars – are not welcome in a parish of four 'villages' where long-standing feuds have embittered people towards their neighbours. They remember the disappointment of the last community worker who has added to the long-standing legacy of disillusionment.

Cynics say 1964–69 were the boom years for the area, but it has undoubtedly got worse since the 1970s. The five coal mines, two steel works, and thriving harbour have all gone. Unemployment averages 20 per cent in Maryport, rising to 28 per cent on Hillside and the next 'village' of Ewanrigg. About half the jobless are long term unemployed.

A survey conducted to define what the community worker could do found the major problems centred on the family, housing, youth, unemployment and apathy. On the Hillside Estate, 20 per cent of the families are single-parent. But there are also many young families where both parents are under twenty-five and out of work.

Many of these families lack basic life skills. They have little idea how to budget on low incomes – 79 per cent of the tenants receive housing benefit. Their diets are poor and women, who get little support from their husbands, lack the ability to care for and stimulate their children. There is an alcoholism problem with

Children in Maryport, 1988.

under-aged drinking by bored and frustrated young people.

But a local neighbourhood project suggests that there is hope that a community worker could make an impact on the area. Funded by the M.S.C. and run by the National Association for the Care and Resettlement of Offenders, the project has identified and acted on a number of local needs, including providing sports days and play days for local children.

It has proved difficult to involve local mothers themselves in the playgroup now up and thriving, but nineteen local people have turned up to special 'chat days' to meet and question housing and welfare officials. With a regular newsletter pushed through their doors, they are at least beginning to receive information about how their lives can be improved.

Mr Diggle says he hopes and expects that the project will lead to 'an improvement in relations across the whole community', across age and class barriers. That has already happened with a similar project in Whitehaven where there was a marked improvement as people have been encouraged and supported to help themselves.

The entire project arose out of the Church's concern, particularly by church members who live in the middle of it all. From the start, the responsibility has been shared with other churches, Mr Diggle says, because the concern was ecumenical.

The partnership, including the local council and the housing association which runs much of the Netherton properties, makes a difference to the project, too. But Mr Diggle is emphatic that it must be a Church based project.

'It is a job which is about the Kingdom,' he says. 'We see it in terms of the spirit of the people and the quality of life in the area. One of the main points of the job will be to maximise the co-operation of the Church members themselves, to involve them as much as possible. It is what the Church should be doing – helping the Church to be a Church.'

Mr Diggle says that some aspects of the job can be done in a secular atmosphere, but there is a determination to bring in a spiritual aspect as well. 'It is my belief that spiritual and material are different aspects of the one unity. You can't have one without the other. My feeling is that there is no cleavage between soul and body in this respect. The Church must be involved where people are. That is the Gospel to me.'

£12,000 has been made available by the Church Urban Fund over two years towards the salary of a community worker to work with families of Maryport.

Winners and losers

Cries of anguish, despair and hopelessness echo through situations such as these. We are forced to become aware that as communities change there are obvious winners and losers. In the material sense some of the accounts of life described in this chapter are about the losers. But how quickly do many of those people turn into winners on their own terms when self-respect is generated and when resources, especially financial support, can be provided from outside? What is so impressive about many of the personal stories told here is that they are about self-help within a supportive community.

Important also is the fact that the Church of England, often with other denominations, is still there. What kind of a local church should it be? We have already seen the hopes of the authors of *Faith in the City* that local Christian communities should be open, participative, outward looking and ecumenical. These characteristics are very much in evidence. Perhaps we could add one other, we have seen a servant church in action.

In these projects Churches, and church members, are quite deliberately out working in the community, alongside those of other faiths and none. Their joint aim is to help restore a sense of self-worth and to rekindle a human spirit often dimmed by the pressures of chance, change and deprivation. All too often the people in the communities described here feel crushed by outside forces and impersonal authorities as England changes around them.

A servant church is there to help sustain and inspire, mind body and spirit – though few working in those areas would think of using such exalted words about themselves. There is a resemblance here to the work of Mother Teresa where she says that when she cares for someone in trouble she knows that she is tending the body of Christ.

4

Homelessness

Few projects supported by the Church Urban Fund fall into one easily defined category. One of the features of a good project which is well earthed in its local community is that it will be trying to meet the hopes of a whole variety of local people. While offering a daytime meeting place for homeless families, the Sebert Road Centre in the London Borough of Newham offers much more as well.

The Sebert Road Centre, Newham

About 700 homeless families have been placed in bed and breakfast hotels by Newham Council. This is an expensive and unsatisfactory option. The Borough has such a major housing problem that it has been forced to fulfil its responsibilities by this course of action.

The closure of several tower blocks which were found to be structurally unsafe has made the problem worse. A day centre for the homeless has been established at Sebert Road. One of the mothers at the Centre, Philomena Hale, nursed her baby daughter, Christina, and said 'If it wasn't for this place, we would have to go miles and miles for somewhere to be safe with the kids'.

Philomena is one of dozens of homeless mums who use the drop-in project at the Sebert Road Centre, which is supported by all 100 churches in the borough. Philomena comes with Christina, 2½ months, and her son Andrew, 16 months, four days a week from 11 a.m. to 2 p.m.

'Homeless people come here to be able to relax, to get away from their hotels and enjoy a friendly atmosphere. You can make tea or coffee, and there's somewhere for the children to play,' she explained.

'In bed and breakfast, there's no room because you're squashed into one room with your kids. Not everyone has cooking facilities in b & b and not a lot of people want to come and see you there either. Even my mum was a bit dubious.

Here, you can get a meal, get the washing done, and get advice about problems with social security from the office.'

As a result of the award of the Church Urban Fund grant, together with a grant from the Methodist Mission Alongside the Poor Fund of £5,000, it was possible to appoint a full-time Centre Manager in September 1988. Mr Cedd Allen-Ambridge, who had previously been working in industry as a computer programmer, has overall responsibility for the management of the various projects using the premises.

He says, 'The church is doing this because there is a need. There are a vast number of homeless people round here – 700 families in bed and breakfast accommodation. Most of them are either confined to their hotels or they are thrown out to walk the streets. If we didn't supply such a centre, no-one else would'.

The Church Urban Fund is paying £12,000 a year for three years towards the salaries of Cedd and other workers at the centre, which also provides training facilities for computer and business studies.

Doorstep: Hull

Jake looked round his light, airy and reasonably furnished attic flatlet and said: 'If I wasn't here, I would still be sleeping in my Mini'.

Jake is 17, unemployed and he has fallen out with his family. His Mini is now off the road – he can't afford to run it any more.

He is just one of many homeless teenagers in Hull to have been rescued from sleeping in garden sheds, bus shelters, abandoned cars or even telephone boxes. In its first two years, the Doorstep project has helped 82 youngsters get permanent housing from the local council. They denied there was a problem.

Doorstep is run by Julia Creasy, the assistant diocesan youth officer for York. An energetic woman who organised ballet, opera and rock festivals during the ten years of fun she had promised herself, before yielding to the call she had first heard at the age of four, she read theology as a mature student.

People working with teenagers on work schemes, through the probation service and the Church realised that homelessness was growing. The youngsters had nowhere to turn to for advice.

People got together and set up an action campaign, carried out a street census, badgered everyone they could think of – from local industry to the local council – to pitch in and help.

'We were told to go away and prove it because nobody believed it,' says Julia. 'But parents were throwing their kids out for financial reasons and the kids wanted to go because of abuse.'

Doorstep started as a charity with a grant from the diocese. It then bought a house financed through the urban programme. The intention was to refurbish it to provide good quality accommodation for single homeless people between the ages of 16 and 18, to demonstrate the need. Then Hull's housing department and local housing associations were supposed to take over.

But Doorstep just grew. It started with one house providing six bedspaces in April 1986. By February 1989, there were 24 bedspaces in five houses, with another 20 houses due to open over the next two years.

'We don't just go for bricks and mortar,' says Julia. 'We provide support which enables young people to mature into adults, able to live independent lives – and the kids make decisions themselves'.

Help includes counselling in 'life and social skills' – anything from making friends to surviving on a shrinking budget, as social security support for young people is cut back.

Steve's first home: one of many teenagers housed by Doorstep, Hull.

The houses are run as hostels with at least a communal living space in each, and someone available each day for advice. Night support workers are now also involved to prevent phone calls in the middle of the night from desperate youngsters.

It's planned that the youngsters spend at least three months in a Doorstep unit before being ready for truly independent living in their own council flat. But some need more time, so they move on to other Doorstep accommodation.

By the beginning of 1989, the staff had increased from two and a half to nine, three of them paid for by the grant of £45,000 from the Church Urban Fund. Julia says this money has allowed Doorstep to develop at a point when it was in danger of collapsing under the strain, and will provide a support worker for the 10-bed houses, a counsellor and administrative help.

Good Shepherd Housing: Wolverhampton

Bushbury in Wolverhampton is one of the most deprived areas in the diocese of Lichfield. Unemployment amongst the male population is 28 per cent, and among males under 25 it is as high as 40 per cent. Overcrowding is high and there are a large number of single parent families.

The Church initiated a community employment scheme for young people in 1981 (Trinity Training Services, already supported by the Fund), and it was from the trainees' experience trying to find accommodation that the housing project was born. The Wolverhampton Youth at Risk Project based in the parish (also supported by the Fund) will work closely with the hostel.

The project consists of four flats provided by the local authority at a reduced rental. The flats can provide accommodation for up to thirteen people; most are referrals from statutory agencies but they also include pastoral contacts.

The hostel is recognised 'as meeting a primary need of the community in housing and resettling the homeless young people'. It is managed by Adullam Homes Housing Association, a Birmingham based Christian association providing central support for a number of church based hostel schemes.

A resident, Dawn, pauses from cooking the tea for the dozen or so other youngsters living in the Good Shepherd housing project. Slowly, she says: 'Before I came here, I was terrified to go out and terrified to come back. It was the burglaries. There were eight burglaries in two years. This place may not be much, but I do feel more secure here. I am still nervous at night when I hear noise.'

And it can be very noisy. The deprived young people living at the hostel often kick in the doors to their own rooms when they have forgotten or lost their keys, even though they have to pay for the damage as well as replacement keys.

Dawn is 23 and she has been living in the hostel for about four months. She heard about it from a neighbour who knew one of the wardens. Until then she was renting a house which she shared with her uncle until he died.

Asked about her own family, Dawn becomes evasive and changes the subject. Many of the young people turning to the hostel for help are alienated from their parents. Dawn is not too sure about some of her fellow residents either. 'I would like to put rat poison in the tea of some of them', she says. 'But Mo won't buy the poison.'

Mo is Maureen Ratcliffe, herself a single parent, who runs the project with Gary Essen who is big enough not to need 'Mo's attitude adjuster' – a baseball bat she jokingly threatens to use to bring the youngsters into line. Mo and Gary both live in the area served by the hostel area and began the project when they realised they were homeless youngsters with severe emotional problems needing help.

Gary Essen, worker at the Good Shepherd hostel, Wolverhampton.

The local council let them have four separate family flats above shops that were on the point of closing down because of vandalism and break-ins. The hostel has probably saved the shops, because the residents deter intruders. But the council charges a normal rent for the flats, which created problems in the beginning because the project had no income but had to find £120 a week. The minute a young person is accepted they are instructed to go and claim income support to pay their way.

The flats have now been converted into hostel accommodation for 10 males and 3 females. There are communal lounges, games room and a launderette is to start soon. The premises and furniture are shabby, but there is hope of better things through prayer cells being formed to help the project.

The intention is that single homeless young people will spend up to six months at the hostel being helped to move on to more independent accommodation. But many of the residents have been there longer because they are not ready to cope on their own. Mo and Gary hope they will be able to open a second-stage hostel later.

Robert, aged 24, has lived at the hostel for more than three years. He dropped out of college and is now on an electronics course through the Employment Training scheme. He has his own room and has become the hostel's handy man, replacing the doors other residents have kicked in.

'I don't know where I would be without this place', he says.

Joe, who is educationally subnormal and was rejected by his father after his mother died, knows where he would be – on the streets or dossing on people's floors. And Ian, who has a severe drink problem, has been kicked out of other hostels because of his drinking.

Mo says the project is special because it is offering a depth of love and care to young people whose problems include glue sniffing, drug abuse and drink that is not offered by anyone else. That is a key reason for the church to be doing it.

She says: 'I know it is what God wants. God wants this place here. He wants in whatever way possible to provide an alternative to the life-style of the kids here. The problems in this area are not going to be solved by whatever government may be in power. We are dealing with cracked up people with cracked up lives'.

The Church Urban Fund is now paying £25,000 over three years for a relief worker to provide cover at night. The policy is never to turn away a young person in genuine need – a distinction drawn to ensure that scarce accommodation is not being used as a temporary night shelter for people who have had a tiff with parents or partners.

East and West London

Homelessness is a continuing problem. Housing of any kind to rent is difficult to find. Hostels and other short-stay accommodation in cities is in short supply. In smaller towns it is non-existent. In the Tower Hamlets Borough of London in 1987 there were over 1,000 homeless people regularly using the four Day Centres there. Since then one Centre has closed and approximately 600 hostel beds have been lost.

The First Step Day Centre at the Tower Hamlets Mission opened in January 1989. It offers a service to the homeless of that area. There are washing facilities, refreshments, there is social work advice, emergency clothing and a furniture store. Also there are regular group meetings to try to help people cope with drug dependency and addiction. There is a weekly service of prayer and healing. A grant of £20,000 over two years has been awarded by the Church Urban Fund towards staffing costs.

The First Step Day Centre in London's East End.

On the other side of the city the West London Day Centre has been offering shelter for London's homeless for the past fourteen years. It is one of the projects of the West London Methodist Mission. It provides day-care facilities for homeless and rootless people over the age of 25. The centre is open every day of the year and visitors number between 100 and 180 per day. Many are long-term homeless people who have spent some time living on the streets of central London.

The Centre includes a canteen, a day room, a craft room with occupational therapy, a room for washing clothes, a medical service and a referral service to help with finding housing. The Church Urban Fund has made a grant of £30,000 over three years towards the salaries of social workers and to enable the Centre to improve its 365 days a year cover.

Chris Wood, from the Centre, says of the aims and life of the place,

'It is a harbour where life's storm damage can be repaired, new stocks and supplies taken on board, new passages sought, and maps and fellow travellers consulted.

It is both a way out and a way in. It is a way out of storm and stress, of homelessness and alcoholism. It is a way in to the resources of the harbour, to food replenishment, and repair, and to new departures.'

St Aidan's, Basford

St Aidan's parish is in the Basford and Bulwell areas of Nottingham. In the winter of 1987, Alan Cooper and Geoff Flowers became worried about the number of trainees on the Y.T.S. scheme who were homeless. They are manager and senior development officer of Job Opportunities Bulwell (J.O.B.) employing around 120 trainees.

'One girl hadn't turned up for work. She had a bed-sit in a rat-infested house in one of the inner areas of Nottingham. She left work and was found "on the streets". Another girl came to work each day with her hair and clothing getting dirtier and dirtier. We found she was breaking into a derelict house each night for shelter. One of the lads was thrown out by his mother "for his own good", she said.'

Faced with twenty-five incidents like this in one year, Alan and

Geoff approached Canon Walter Beasley, Rector of St Mary's, Bulwell, and Chair of Job Opportunities, Bulwell. The church council responded and, after discussions with Nottingham City Housing Department, resolved to rent a near-derelict house in Bulwell and accommodate six homeless girls.

Changing circumstances and opposition from people in the area forced the church council to withdraw its plans. But they continued to pray and soon they were able to find lodging for seven homeless lads in a caring, private home.

When the suggestion came that St Mary's, Bulwell, and St Aidan's, Basford, might work together as a team, they planned for a new hostel to be built onto the unfinished east end of St Aidan's Church.

The architect's square-metre cost was £140,000, but using the trainees at J.O.B. meant it could be done for £90,000. The trainees' work in building, joinery, decorating and sewing has already shown how high their standards are. It is also of great benefit to the young people if they are given resources to help other young people with their problems.

The plan is that each room will have built-in furniture on the pattern of a student bed-sit. Full board will be available where necessary and there will be a live-in housekeeper to oversee the hostel.

The Church Urban Fund has contributed £50,000 towards St Aidan's – an imaginative and cost-effective scheme.

St Basil's Centre, Birmingham

At a conservative estimate at least 5,000 young people become homeless in Birmingham each year. St Basil's Centre, founded in 1964 as an experimental youth centre for work with alienated young people, accommodates between 800–900 young people each year. 1,000 are given intensive help, 12,000 are given information and advice, through the Kiosk and The Link.

The work of the Centre is likely to face large cuts by the City Council although no decision has yet been made, but as a general policy decision they do not wish to fund advice and information centres.

These are currently staffed by a project manager and three members of staff, one of whom is a resettlement worker, the other two are housing aid workers.

In recent months they have rehoused every young person who

has sought help through building up an extensive network. This enables young people to be moved into appropriate accommodation whether night shelters, hostels, landlords or through negotiations which allow them to return home.

The Church Urban Fund has made a grant of £24,000 to help finance the Kiosk, so that the vital welfare rights and information service can continue to function, helping people like Lee James who spoke of his experience at the Coventry Service for the Church Urban Fund in September 1989,

'You lose your self-respect and you lose your trust in people. Your ability to communicate with people becomes strained, as you feel let down and rejected.

People take advantage of you, especially if you are young.

I found it really hard to trust anyone, even people who wanted to help me.

I thank God that I found St Basil's or I probably wouldn't have been here today.'

All the C.U.F.'s £18 million would not solve England's housing problem – far from it. What it can do is provide publicity, money and encouragement to those courageous people who are keeping the problem in the public eye and who are doing quite amazing work with great self-sacrifice in their local areas. They are still there when the issues raised by Christmas appeals are forgotten by the rest of us for another year.

5

Young Adults

Many young people in inner-city areas have had a bad experience of school. Truanting is a feature of life. A very high percentage of small scale crime is committed by school age children. Projects supported by the Fund aim, in a very limited way, to encourage young people trying to work with these issues.

Work with teenagers can be very rewarding when real progress can be seen. It can equally be very dispiriting when high hopes are dashed, when promises are not kept and youngsters go their own way.

It is important to remember that the disappointments and let-downs are often caused by wrong expectations. That the behaviour of many teenagers arises out of difficult home circumstances and a lack of a sense of worth derived from school life. Dress and behaviour which will exclude many from the immediate possibility of work, if any is to be had, are an external protest at life in a world which has seemed more like a punishment than a gift.

Many of the projects in this chapter are small in scale. Some describe discovering the local small group life of teenagers and trying to get alongside in whatever ways are possible. Other pieces of work are in one-to-one relationships. It takes a lot of time and care to help restore self-confidence and confidence in a seemingly uncaring society. It takes vision, optimism and limitless enthusiasm to keep the work going. Youth workers of all ages and all generations will understand and empathise with the accounts in this chapter and will realise what a tremendous boost these comparatively generous sums of money from the C.U.F. can be to a threatened youth work project.

The nature of the life of many teenagers is that they would never admit to the benefits of what has been made available. It is only when they have gone on to the next stage of life that they will begin to live what they have been helped to experience. They will never have heard of the Church Urban Fund.

Among the most severely disadvantaged are Afro-Caribbean youngsters, especially girls. The work of the Redemption Drop-In Centre is characteristic in its way of trying to work alongside these young people.

41

Redemption Drop-In Centre, London N15

Redemption, Lealand Road, Stamford Hill in North London is a training project for 37 young people each doing a 21 hour week over a period of twelve months, more hours would affect their benefits. The Project Manager is Ben Bentum, originally from Ghana, and the Project Co-ordinator is Pastor 'Rocky' Scott, originally from Jamaica. The project was set-up after research into the supposed 'apathy' of the young towards making use of training opportunities.

Ben Bentum says the research showed that many young women were unable to take advantage of training programmes because nearly all of them were single mothers 'saddled with children'. The high cost of child minding – £30 to £40 a week – combined with the low incomes they could expect made it not worth their while going to work. Bentum blames their potentially low wages on the lack of a minimum wage in Britain and says they are better off claiming housing, child and supplementary benefit than working.

The research found that another barrier was the inflexibility of most existing courses. The structure and organisation of colleges and polytechnics are too rigid; you have to report at specific times on particular days, and most students cannot fit into that. So, says Bentum, the project designed a programme with the needed flexibility, building in the one-to-one training that many of the students needed because of their varying strengths and weaknesses.

The programme takes a different approach in other ways, too. Students, says Bentum, want to be regarded as participants being helped rather than trainees on the receiving end of a formal teacher/student relationship. This is particularly important when the experience of racial prejudice has made many young blacks bitter against the system and anyone who is purveyor of training and advice. They might well respond to offers of help with the cry 'where were you when I needed you to stop me stealing' because they now feel the system has criminalised them.

'Every human being, no matter the level of your skills or competence, has potential,' says Bentum.

The project does its own recruitment and originally had 30 places approved by the former M.S.C. All places were filled within six weeks of the start – which is rare. There is now a waiting list and the project is allowed to increase its places to 40.

The project provides counselling before anyone is taken on.

They attempt to build up an almost parental relationship with the students. Bentum says that many of them have never had a caring parent and their reality is living their lives on the street, in the gutter, in the ghetto. Their friends don't know any better than they do. 'So we give them that first hope' that there is someone willing to listen to them.

The next stage is confidence building, starting with helping them to identify their problems and difficulties. 'We don't tell them what their problems are, but force them to examine their own problems' through a process of self analysis, self examination and self assessment.

Bentum says: 'All the time they put all the blame on the government, their parents, teachers, or – if they have worked – on their employers. They see nothing wrong with themselves. We hold up a double mirror to look at the two sides of themselves. Gradually we lead them to realise that at least part of the problem was caused by themselves'.

Then they are helped to find solutions to the problems they have discovered; again they make their own decisions – wrong ones are seen as part of the learning process. An individual time-table is designed to help them achieve it. The training is geared towards City & Guilds and R.S.A. certificates 'there are too many facilities for games playing in this country and not enough for intellectual discussion' says Bentum.

In the project's first mock exams, based on R.S.A. papers, 80 per cent of students passed numeracy and basic maths, and 65 per cent passed English.

English and maths are compulsory subjects; students can also choose hairdressing, electronics, book-keeping and office skills with computer science as a core subject. They want to extend into other areas: building, plumbing, motor mechanics, etc. Four young people have been found jobs before completing their course. A major problem remains – funding has yet to be found for the computer studies tutor's salary. Haringey council has declined because it has no money. The Church Urban Fund has made a capital grant of £11,800 to provide computer equipment so that trainees can gain experience of the kind of equipment which they will meet when they get a job. Rocky Scott says many of the youngsters have never touched computers before but 'everyone is so positive'. They are not necessarily so enthusiastic about his attempts to build better relationships with the police though. They are sometimes regarded as 'pro police' by the black community, but

Students at the Redemption drop-in centre in Tottenham, north London.

those coming to the regular meetings set up with the police since Broadwater Farm come to the opposite conclusion.

Scott says his initiative arose out of the tension between the police and the black community which was affecting even the most innocent. He had discussions with other church leaders and senior police officers when it looked as if there might be another riot because of the provocative attitude of some policemen. The police response was speedy; they said that they had already attended too many meetings organised by blacks at which they were always attacked. Scott persevered, organised another meeting at which 'tenseness was there' but the police came up with several positive proposals. The Christian Police Association, now directly involved in church meetings, emerged out of a seminar. Scott says the main intention was to break down the black view that all white people and police are evil and: 'We wanted to demonstrate that people should be taken as found. We wanted to demonstrate to the white community that not all black people are criminals, evil or lazy as alleged'.

There are now monthly meetings and both local police superintendents have been to talk to the students – who let them know in no uncertain terms how they felt about the police. There have also been attempts to make sure that admitted 'black haters' among young officers who 'use their heads' come to meetings. Scott is convinced that the education thus given to these bobbies is informative and helping to build better understandings. And the kids are also learning about the problems the police face.

Pastor Rocky says, 'When I read the scriptures I see the pattern of Jesus Christ is one that was concerned about humanity. A great deal of my philosophy was born out by Martin Luther King – his commitment, dedication and his willingness to give his life for humanity. I realised that for us to function as a church goes beyond preaching behind a pulpit. It is not the people in the church that are rioting, hating, but people outside. I believe they have justifiable reason to hate, but Martin Luther King preached that non-violence is the way forward; he said that if we all say 'an eye for an eye' we will all end up as blind people with no-one to help each other. I believe that if the Church is strong we can stand up and demonstrate loving one's enemy – doing exactly what Jesus Christ says. Not easy to tell these youngsters who are not committed to Christianity, but I am so encouraged at how they have responded'.

Stockton Anchorage

Stockton Anchorage was begun in 1982. It aims to work alongside unemployed young people by providing social, recreational and leisure facilities. It also tries to provide low-cost housing and direct employment for those with little experience of work. The Church Urban Fund supports the employment of the Centre's co-ordinator, Terry Bayford, a Church Army Captain. A revenue grant of £55,750 has been awarded over five years.

Terry Bayford explains that most of the youngsters taking up the 70 Employment Training places there belong to a local culture where it doesn't occur to them to apply for jobs. Up to 70 per cent of men on some nearby estates are jobless. Young people have no experience of a nine-to-five existence or having to be in the same place at the same time every day. So he is very proud that a quarter of the youngsters taking part in the project's environmental scheme left for permanent jobs.

Steve Leach spent three months in Kenya in 1988 – with Operation Raleigh. He helped to build two schools for the local Masai children, charted unexplored jungle, trekked across the desert on a camel and picked up a few words of Swahili. Yet Steve is unemployed and homeless. He won the trip through endurance and survival tests in competition with 96 other youngsters.

Steve is 22. He hasn't worked since leaving school. He is one of the many youngsters involved with the Anchorage project in Stockton, which takes its name partly from Stockton Borough Council's emblem. But there's also another meaning: stability for the sort of jobless young people that most other agencies reject.

Young people are encouraged to set up their own businesses – an idea pioneered by the Anchorage long before either local authorities or industry thought of it, according to Revd David Whittington, the local Anglican vicar. So far, about ten young people have tried to start their own business at the Anchorage: two of them are still going. Denis Briggs runs a picture framing business, now based in a nearby shop. Shaw has taken over the coffee bar at the Anchorage. Among the so-called 'failures', is a lad whose work on his arts and design business led to a permanent full-time job with the county council.

The Church Urban Fund's agreement to pay Terry's salary for the next five years ensures the project's 'most important provision', according to David Whittington. The breathing space offered by these five years will be used to make sure alternative funding is available when the Church Urban Fund money runs out.

He's sure the Church should be involved to fill a gap not being met by the official services, and more importantly, it offers an informal and non-threatening approach. Many of these young people can't cope with the formality of official bureaucracy and so without support from the Anchorage, are never able to realise their full potential.

Terry Bayford concludes 'If they can spend 52 weeks here and go away able to be punctual, have good working relationships with themselves and other people, and respond to "authority" by being willing to get on with it, we will give them a good work record for the future'.

Video Vault: Southwark

Mitcham Lane Baptist Church is situated in a multi-racial, residential area, bordering Tooting, Mitcham and Streatham. The area, which includes two large council estates, is described as an educational priority area. The closest school is Graveney Secondary school which services 1800 pupils, many of whom are of Asian origin with English as their second language. Mitcham Lane Baptist Church already has links with this school and it was thought that a large proportion of pupils would be attracted to the idea of a 'Video Vault'.

46

This provides a meeting place on the premises of the old Baptist Church which is no longer used for worship. It enables young people to take part in a fast moving, multi media show, comprising videos, live music, drama, competitions, games and talks on current issues. It provides community leaders with a platform to meet and talk to the young people of the area. The 'Video Vault' is a community event and is not 'overtly evangelistic'. It has the support of the two local Anglican churches.

The Video Vault is staffed by a Young Worker at the Baptist Church who has been seconded to the church for a period of two years from January 1988.

The Video Vault is a lively and imaginative project which aims to get alongside teenagers and to enter into their culture. No ordinary youth club, and in a multi-racial area, here the churches are making a real attempt to serve young people in the community in an area where 'conventional' church activities would have no impact at all. £5,000 was contributed by the C.U.F. to the Video Vault for the purchase of equipment.

All Saints, Brixton

Another of the ten projects initially supported by the Fund in the Southwark Diocese is the youth project of All Saints Church, Lytham Road, Clapham Park.

This multi-racial area suffers severe deprivation – it has the highest incidence of infant mortality in the country, 14 per cent of the housing stock lacks basic amenities. Although overall unemployment for the area is 20 per cent it is as high as 50–60 per cent amongst the Afro-Caribbean population.

There is great concern about young people growing up here. It is generally agreed that 'club-based' youth work is now inappropriate in the inner cities so an experimental youth project, based on a new approach pioneered in Cambridge, has been set up.

The main emphasis of the Project is to recognise the natural groupings and meetings of young people and to operate within these small units rather than within the traditional youth club setting.

It is based on the Church of England parish, but is run in close liaison with the Methodist and Pentecostal churches. The Fund has provided £45,000 over three years towards the salary of a project leader.

'The Warren' Resource Centre, Hull

The application to the Fund stated that Hull is the third most violent city in the country and has one of the three worst outer-city estates.

The Warren is a community resource centre for 16–25 year olds, a group for which unemployment is running at 10 per cent. The aim of The Warren is to assist young people in Hull to gain the confidence and skills necessary to enable them to play a fuller role in society. In addition to counselling a very wide range of activities for young people takes place at The Warren.

Since 1982 when the Warren opened there has been an increasing demand for counselling on a wide range of issues and problems, so the Warren has a Youth Counsellor who has developed high quality provision and some innovative work of national importance. A feature of the work is that many of the 'clients' become volunteers, and are trained to help various aspects of the project's work. This often leads to employment or further education.

There is an urgent need for further Counselling/Outreach workers to work alongside him, and to develop the work with young homeless, and address the problems of drunkenness and violence among the young in the centre of Hull. The C.U.F. has made a revenue grant of £20,581 over three years.

Although this project is not managed by a church organisation, it is regarded as of great importance by the Diocese who provide £13,500 towards the salary and overhead costs of The Warren. The project is also supported by the Midland Bank. The Warren is run in close co-operation with Doorstep, Hull, described in the chapter on homelessness.

The Burnside Centre, Manchester

The Burnside Centre is situated on the Langley estate in Middleton, originally built as a Manchester overspill estate to rehouse residents of the so called North Manchester slum areas. The estate has now lost its status and become a fringe part of Metropolitan Rochdale although it is owned by Manchester Housing Authority. Many of the houses are empty, awaiting repair and renovation. The shops, including the main shopping mall, appear semi-derelict. The roll of the community school for 11–14 year olds has fallen from 700 to 150. The clergy, members of the Community of the Glorious Ascension, and staff of the Burnside Centre are the only professional people willing to live on the estate.

Brother David and Brother Simon of the Community of the Glorious Ascension, workers at the Burnside Centre.

The Centre is used for community meetings and activities, youth work and occasional worship. There is a youth club on five evenings a week with an average attendance of 60. On five mornings a week there is a mother and toddler group. On one afternoon a week there is 'Day-space' – a range of activities for unemployed young adults. The Centre is also used for local councillors' surgeries, children's parties, local action committee meetings (community police liaison, homewatch), area youth service events, etc. An average of 20 young people a year seek sanctuary in the building before returning to their family home.

The Burnside Centre is at a point of crisis because of the state of the building which now needs extensive repairs. The job of making plans for the redevelopment of the building has provoked strong community support. They are now looking to the future with fresh vision and enthusiasm.

The Fund has made a capital grant of £30,000 towards the refurbishment of this building.

Aston Community Youth Project, Birmingham

Aston was 'broken as a proud, long-established industrial community of 40,000 people by the bulldozers and slum clearance of the 1970s and industrial recessions of the 1980s'. It is characterised by 'inadequate access to or take-up by children and young people of opportunities that exist in the wider neighbourhood'.

The application to the Fund was submitted by 'The Voice of the People Trust' in conjunction with 'Handsworth Breakthrough' and 'Aston Churches Working Together'. The project which was researched for eighteen months aims to set up a detached community youth project with two full-time workers and volunteer help.

The workers will make contact with young people who are not effectively involved in sport or leisure activities or youth clubs. They might for example make contact with a local graffiti gang with the object of weaning them away from vandalism. They will aim to wean youngsters away from vandalism and try to channel their energies into creative projects so that they can discover the sense of achievement which comes from doing things well.

The Project Leader would be a physical training instructor skilled in sports and leisure activities, including survival skills training, outward bound and mountain leadership. The Community Youth Leader would be skilled in detached youth work and in creative activities such as the arts or social and community service. They would work together as a small team setting up volunteer help, making links with local youth organisations, arranging sporting and cultural activities, linking young people in to established groups.

The total cost of this project is estimated to be £102,770. The C.U.F. has made a considerable contribution towards the salaries of the two workers of £75,000 over three years. The Eagle Star Insurance Group is also supporting the project.

Youth at Risk, Wolverhampton

David and Lynne Hyde are Christians committed to helping young people in Wolverhampton. Their work started some years ago by opening their home 24 hours a day to any young person experiencing problems.

Problems encountered included family breakdown, drug and alcohol abuse, homelessness, unemployment, pregnancy and violence. The majority of young people visiting them were 'bikers'. As

Dave and Lynne had been 'bikers' themselves in the late sixties and early seventies they were able to relate to their culture and this eased the way to counselling.

The aim now is to establish this work by setting up a Christian Coffee Bar in the town centre of Wolverhampton. The Local Authority has found suitable premises above some shops which will be let for a very reasonable rent; they will also be prepared to help with refurbishing the furnishing.

Lynn and Dave Hyde from Youth at Risk, Wolverhampton.

The aims are to offer counselling, welfare advice and emergency help to young people in need. All paid staff and certain volunteers will receive training in this. Other support such as prison and hospital visiting will also be given. Various recreational facilities will be offered. The Fund has made a grant of £15,000 towards the setting up costs of Youth at Risk. The building was opened on 13 May 1989 and now has 130–140 visitors per week. Sue, a regular visitor says,

'It's great to be here. It feels great to have someone to talk to. I don't know what I would have done without it because I was

51

getting in such a state because of my nerves. The atmosphere at home was affecting my nerves and putting a strain on my relationships with others. But here there's always someone to talk to. I come most days either at morning or at night.'

Each of these projects demonstrates the care and cautiousness required when working with young people. The descriptions of local situations are graphic and convey the atmosphere of a world which is closed to adults and away from the experience of most of the population.

Funding for the continuation of youth work projects is always difficult as less money than ever becomes available from local authorities. The best pieces of youth work done by the churches in recent years have been in co-operation with other organisations. There is always the hope, or temptation, that good youth work will somehow bring youngsters into congregations. It is wrong that such a hope should exist at all and a great bonus when an active faith does begin to grow. Self-interest in youth work will be sensed immediately by youngsters and is a recipe for disaster.

6

(Un) Employment

Almost every Diocese in England could have made an application to the Fund for work with unemployed people. In many Dioceses such projects have been running for ten or more years. Changes in government training schemes and their provision and funding generate as many demands for support as do innovatory ideas.

Across the country different kinds of people are unemployed. Reasons for this often stem from the history of an area. In regions which have been prosperous with traditional industries there has frequently been widespread devastation. The decline of shipbuilding in the North East, the closure of pits in the mining area there and in South Yorkshire, the virtual collapse of many parts of the engineering industry in the West Midlands, have all brought great suffering. The decline of Liverpool as a port has changed the nature of that city.

The recession of the mid-1970s made it particularly difficult for young people to get jobs. Afro-Caribbean youngsters were among the hardest hit. In many areas girls have had particular problems. The situation in the 1990s is going to be different. There will still be areas with high unemployment for particular reasons. The dramatic decline in the number of young people will mean that their skills will be in great demand. Training and retraining will become increasingly important. Specialist support will always be needed for those who find it difficult, for whatever reason, to fit into a regular pattern of work.

The Lichfield Diocese in the West Midlands is a place where many engineering companies provide parts for the motor industry. Recent decline has meant that many skilled people, as well as teenagers, have found themselves without work. Consequently the Diocese appointed a full-time worker to co-ordinate projects and to assist parishes and groups in their applications for funding.

Roapp Hall, Darlaston

Rubery Owen, which once employed 10,000 and was a byword for industrial paternalism in the West Midlands, sold a building that used to be a training hall for apprentices – Roapp Hall. It is now a charity that provides a much needed resource centre in a town with nearly 30 per cent male unemployment.

Harry, made redundant at 61 after forty-seven years working for Rubery Owen, comes into Roapp Hall every day to eat a meal of meat and two veg and a sweet for 65p.

'I enjoy cooking – my mother made sure that all of us could take care of ourselves and it meant I wasn't totally lost when my wife died,' he says. 'But you couldn't put a meal like this together yourself at that cost.'

He's one of about two dozen pensioners who regularly come to Roapp Hall for their lunches, made by other redundant and unemployed men and women who volunteer for training in basic catering skills. Benefit rules mean that the trainee cooks are unpaid and can only work 20 hours a week, which limits the scope of their training.

The advantage for them is gaining confidence and the rudiments of a marketable skill in a town that has become an industrial wasteland. Half of the trainees, whose ages range from 17 to the 60s, have gone on to either catering jobs or college courses since the scheme began in July 1987.

As well as lunches, Roapp Hall provides lists of job vacancies, updated daily when the supervisor goes to the nearest Job Centre nearly five miles away. There is no local Citizens Advice Bureau, so a welfare rights worker gives help with benefits. There is a snack bar whose speciality is an all-day breakfast of amazing proportions, and a range of other activities for local people, including bingo sessions for pensioners and women's groups. The Hall now wants to make a special effort to help disabled people.

Both the trainees and the regular diners owe their opportunities to the initiative of a group of redundant people who decided in 1981 to pool their redundancy money to provide some kind of resource centre for the unemployed. The group, who dubbed themselves Darlaston Redundancy Action Group, won the support of the industrial chaplain, local Methodists, local business and the National Coal Board.

Although the Hall's activities are based on the values of community service, its existence has helped a number of people to gain the confidence to find jobs elsewhere. Yet much of the work has been threatened by the change of emphasis of the Manpower Services Commission.

The M.S.C. pays for the Hall's staff who are all Community Programme workers. C.P. work must be based on training rather than community service even where it has been shown to be successful in enabling people to find jobs. The Church Urban Fund has been asked to step in and help with funding.

The other side of Roapp Hall's work has a more certain future – factory start-up units for new businesses. Like the catering course, these help people of all ages.

First man in was Alan Silvester, made redundant after 40 years as a pattern maker with HF Lloyds. He now makes nursery furniture for schools and playgroups. His child-size washing machines and microwave ovens are crafted lovingly from high quality birch plywood, beech and mahogany and would grace the nursery of any stately home.

Dawn Forbes, aged 22, and Stuart Merrifield, 24, have set up an enamelling factory together after spending years on Government programmes without ever finding work. They make framed enamel pictures from ceramic transfers, and have sold 150 pieces to the gift shop at Blenheim Palace.

Richard Dunk, 34, makes armour. He used to do it at home but the noise and the lack of space were restricting. He landed the contract for the 300th anniversary of the Armada, an English Heritage project which organised displays all over Devon and Cornwall.

Stephen Rawling, rector of St Lawrence's, Darlaston, chairs the Roapp Hall committee and is firmly committed to the church's role in its work. Fifteen years ago, 25,000 people were employed in Darlaston; now there are only 2,500. All the large employers – Rubery Owen, Guest Keen & Nettlefolds – have gone.

The blow, he says, was worse because there was no experience in formerly thriving Darlaston of unemployment. This town was cushioned even in the 1930s, and local people had no idea about how to tighten their belts and make do when hard times came.

'People were just rocked on their feet because the world changed overnight,' Mr Rawling said, 'I have had to take a number of funerals of suicides because people couldn't face it any more. It was just devastating.'

Roapp Hall was born out of that despair when those made redundant wanted to use their nest egg to provide 'a base, a resource for a town that had had its heart taken out'.

The Church Urban Fund has made a grant of £25,000 over three years towards the cost of running the Roapp Hall project. It will help pay the salary of a manager and will enable factory units to be rented at a price which will help in the first two years of starting up a business.

Trinity Training Services, Bushbury, Wolverhampton

Trinity Training Services is based in North Wolverhampton, the Low Hill and Bushbury areas. These have both high unemployment and high crime rates. The decline of local industry has had its effect and there are poor housing conditions. There is apathy amongst the community, which affects the attitudes of the young people, many of whom have special needs. This has always been the main catchment area for trainees.

Since Youth Training Scheme sponsors have had to obtain Approved Training Organisation status, many small church-based Y.T.S. schemes have had to close. Because unemployment among young Afro Caribbean people in Wolverhampton can rise as high as 90 per cent in some areas, Lichfield Diocese felt it wrong to pull out of this work. They therefore encouraged the merging of a Methodist, Anglican and Y.W.C.A. scheme in 1986 to form Trinity Training Services.

The overall aim of the project is to train young people to assist in their transition to working life. This not only involves job training, but also personal effectiveness and social skills which in turn affect attitudes to the community. The aim is to help people in this deprived urban area, to find and implement ways of meeting the spiritual and material needs of their own community.

A trainee, Joanne Twiss, paused and said: 'If I wasn't here, I'd be on the dole. A friend of mine did that for eight weeks and she couldn't stand it. It was *so* boring'.

Joanne, aged 17, is one of about 100 young people on a two-year printing course at T.T.S. She's a classic example of what the agency tries to do – prepare youngsters for the world of work and encourage girls to go for non-traditional jobs. Printing is still largely a male world.

The 16–18 year-olds at T.T.S. come from areas which are renowned as being deprived and dangerous. Not surprisingly, they appear unpromising job material. The local community is so close knit that they don't even like using the frequent bus services to take a 10-minute ride into town to look for work.

Yet, in 1988, there was an 89 per cent success rate – only four of the forty-seven trainees who completed their two-year courses

Learning to work at Trinity Training Services, Wolverhampton.

didn't find work. Even taking into account the drop-outs who left after a year, the overall success rate is 57 per cent.

T.T.S. offers training in six areas: printing, catering, building work, woodwork, horticulture and social and community care. The trainees spend three months, sometimes more, at Trinity before being placed in a local company.

Nearly a quarter of the trainees are black, reflecting their proportion in the local community. One is Stephen Phillips, 18, a star trainee in the catering group. He had to drop out of a college catering course because he couldn't afford to pay for the cooking ingredients.

'But there is a higher standard here anyway,' he said, and adds that he gets on with both the trainees at Trinity and the staff.

Trinity's horticultural programme, recovering from an early setback when its entire stock of conifers was stolen, is now about to expand. Karen Jones, the manager, approached Chilington Hall, a nearby stately home for advice – and was rewarded by being offered the free use of nearly an acre of land. This will be used for training and for producing vegetables, flowers and plants for sale.

Catering and printing trainees already contribute to fund raising by offering their skills – they have catered for a garden party and sell posters and other printing services. Although these are comparatively cheap, there is no intention of undercutting commercial firms. 'We are here to create work, not to take it away,' the staff insist. 'We are offering services to people who could not afford commercial prices.'

The trio of previous agencies from which Trinity was formed were all church-based, including Methodists and a Y.W.C.A. scheme. Money from the Church Urban Fund has been used to refurbish the building and get the project off the ground with new equipment.

'If we had had to pay for all of it ourselves, we would not be viable now,' says Karen.

Karen describes the commitment expected at T.T.S. 'During their training, the trainees must spend time working alongside employers. The employers we use are called Placement Providers. The scheme has developed many placements in and around the Wolverhampton area, but are continually seeking new and effective placements to widen our scope and improve training.'

Another requirement of the scheme is that during the first year trainees must spend at least 13 weeks at 'off the job' training relevant to their training area, which at present takes place at either Bilston Community College, Sandwell College, Henry Boot, or Matthew Boulton College of Printing. This takes the form of either day release college terms or three weeks block courses. During the second year, trainees must spend at least seven weeks 'off the job' training in the workshops.

The Lichfield Diocese purchased T.T.S.'s new factory unit at a cost of £70,000. The Tudor Trust and British Gas also support the project. The Church Urban Fund has made a grant of £21,515 to assist with the purchase of catering and printing equipment.

The Advent Project, Birkenhead

The Advent project is an employment initiative of the Society of St Vincent de Paul, an international charity largely supported by lay members of the Roman Catholic and some Anglican churches.

The Advent project helps in areas where the unemployment rate is three times the national average. As well as money from the St Vincent de Paul Society, the Catholic newspaper, *The Universe*, has given its support. The idea was launched at the annual meeting of the Society in Scarborough in the autumn of 1988. The appeal was launched in the Advent of 1988 – hence its name – with the slogan that 'All the unemployed want for Christmas is a job'. It is now a fully registered charity. The Urban Fund was at first cautious in its support of this principally Catholic charity but has decided to go ahead as a strong measure of inter-denominational support. The first piece of work is based in Birkenhead and Mike Kennedy, the Project Director, says:

'Our aim is simple. We believe the statutory bodies are not coping sufficiently with the unemployment problem. We believe that our Churches have the local community involvement, commitment and trust to be able to directly help the most disadvantaged.

Being in a deprived community where unemployment runs at two or three times the national average, up to 30 per cent or more, usually means your personal confidence is sapped, you shun "officialdom", you need motivating, you need to have your horizons opened to enable you to help yourself.'

The Advent Project helps unemployed individuals set themselves up in business under the Government's Enterprise Allowance scheme.

Tom Elcock was 58 when he was made redundant from the printing firm where he had worked for 27 years. He was unemployed for twelve months before the S.V.P. contacted him. 'I kept looking for jobs, but unfortunately my age seemed to be against me. The help offered by the Advent Project was "a godsend".'

'Going down the dole office, I used to feel "This is wrong",' he says. 'The sad thing, the thing that hurt me most, was seeing so many young people down there.'

Tom Elcock now has his own business, Chameleon Art, which he runs from the front room of his home in Birkenhead. He trained as a Commercial Artist after leaving school, and is now putting his training to good use, producing designs, displays, illustrations and paintings.

His most recent commission was from the Mowlem construction company who asked Tom to design the company Christmas card. He has also produced some of the designs for the Advent Project literature.

Paul Kelly and Mark Richards represent the other end of the unemployment spectrum in Birkenhead. Both 20, they have known each other since they were five and neither of them has had a full-time paid job since they left Bishop Challoner High School in 1985.

They, too, now have their own company, Advent Electronics. Based in a room above a shop, they assemble electronic circuit boards for burglar and fire alarms.

Their latest project is the research and development of a Biocide Dosing Unit, for use in cooling towers, to stop the spread of Legionnaire's Disease.

Their love of electronic gadgetry dates back to their schooldays, and their knowledge and experience comes from the various Youth Training Schemes in which they have been involved.

'There was no hope of me getting a job in electronics,' says Paul who heard about the Advent Project when he met the manager, Mike Kennedy after helping out at the S.V.P. summer camp.

The project has been particularly helpful, they say, in providing advice about grants and business contacts. 'Large companies wouldn't be interested in helping people like us,' says Mark.

Being on the Enterprise Allowance scheme, and having the support and advice of the Advent Project, has meant that they will be masters of their own destiny. 'We'll be able to plan our future,' says Mark, 'instead of living from day to day like you do on the dole.'

Peter Voice, 31, had been unemployed for eighteen months before he became involved with the Advent Project. 'It was absolutely soul-destroying,' he says.

Now, with Wayne Humphries, 25, and John Lovett, 21, he is the co-owner of Leisurekraft, a workers' co-operative manufacturing fibreglass canoes. Since setting up business in an out-building of a friends' house, they have made seven canoes. The three met on a Community Programme scheme where they were taught how to make the canoes. Peter realised he couldn't face going back on the dole. 'I had to do something,' he says. 'There was no way that I was going to go back on the dole.'

Their canoes sell for £130, which they hope is within the reach of people on low budgets and groups such as youth clubs and scout groups. 'We like to feel we're putting something back into the community,' says Peter.

For the three budding businessmen, the help of Mike Kennedy and the Advent Project has been vital to the success of their enterprise, particularly the marketing advice.

The three are slowly getting used to the idea of being their own boss. 'We're loving it because no matter how hard it gets for us, the rewards are basically our own,' says Peter.

They are confident about the future. Leisurekraft is set to

expand with plans to manufacture fibreglass trailer bodies, and weather protection shields for motorcycles.

For John, the youngest of the partners: 'This is a chance in a million to work for ourselves, instead of working for someone else and getting exploited.'

Money for the Birkenhead Advent Project, £24,000 over three years from the Church Urban Fund, will be matched by an equal sum from the Catholic Church.

The Dearne Valley Venture, Sheffield

Another ecumenical project which has come to the Fund for support is the Dearne Valley Venture in an area between Barnsley, Rotherham and Sheffield. The application to the Fund came from the Anglican Deanery of Wath, together with the local Methodist Circuit and Roman Catholic Deanery.

The Dearne Valley was the heartland of the South Yorkshire Coalfield; in 1961 over 15,600 people worked in fourteen pits; now only 3,500 work in just four of them. The accelerated closures and reductions in staffing in the 1970s, together with their knock-on effects on the local economy, meant that by 1979 the Dearne Valley had an unemployment rate of 20 per cent.

From 1981 the decline in the economy of the Dearne Valley became acute. Since the 1984–85 Miner's Strike no less than six pits have closed. These closures, together with further reductions in the working pits, have meant a loss of over 3,680 jobs. Other industries, never very substantial in the area, have suffered too. Nearly 300 jobs have been lost in just three of the larger clothing firms and the closure of United Glass in April 1988 brought a further 500 job losses. The three towns in the south of the valley lost no fewer than 1,200 jobs in the space of one months.

It is small exaggeration to say that the economy of the Dearne Valley is now virtually destroyed. Apart from the four remaining coal mines, three of which have large question marks over them, the valley has now neither any major industrial plant nor anything approaching a network of minor industrial or commercial concerns. The present pattern of government grant-aid fails to give the valley any edge over more attractive areas in South Yorkshire and all three local authorities are experiencing enormous difficulty in bringing any new industry into the area.

The Dearne Valley Venture has grown out of Wath Deanery's initiative eight years ago to propose that the Diocese of Sheffield had an Unemployment Officer, who would concentrate on practical work in that deanery. This was subsequently followed up with spiritual support, money and resources. Similar help soon came also from the local Methodist Circuit, from many individual church members from different denominations, and from the community at large.

Creative activity lies at the root of what is now a network of small-scale 'shoe-string' workshops and centres. Rock music, printing, clothes-making, crafts, writing are well established; photography, pottery, keyboard skills have begun; others are in the pipeline. The new mini-centres are for meeting, eating, planning events, buying and selling. And a small centre has begun to preserve, for the next generation, the disappearing culture of this former mining valley.

This network has sprung up as a result of the work of Michael Keen, the Diocesan Unemployment Officer. These are not church initiated projects in the usual sense but involve church members in their capacity as members of the community.

Their aim is to foster self-confidence in the unemployed and wherever possible it is intended that the centres should become self-supporting.

Michael Keen, the Unemployment Officer, has moved on to new work and an application is being made for a Project Co-ordinator to continue the work with the Dearne Valley Venture. This work will include:

1. Supporting groups to run projects, enabling them to grow and develop and establish sources of income.
2. Developing expertise in the network in fundraising and resources, developing a strategy for the continuation of the projects and to reviewing the options for the future of the Dearne Valley Venture.
3. Supporting the other paid workers in the network.

When Chris Hallam, the Fund's Field Officer, visited the Venture to assess the application for the Fund in September 1988, he wrote,

'My visit today with the Diocesan Development Officer, Ian McCollough, started appropriately enough at Cortonwood which is a contact centre and craft group and advice point. A good lunch is provided here for anyone who cares to call at a cost of 85p. An excellent lunch is provided on every weekday and the kitchen have a staff of three, all voluntary workers.

Over lunch we had the opportunity of meeting one or two of the helpers and also Reverend Richard Pamplin, Chairman of the D.V. Council, and Reverend Nick Jowell, Vicar of Brampton.

Our first stop after lunch was a quick look at the Look-In information and advice centre which is a portacabin in a carpark in Wath-upon-Dearne!

Our next stop was at the Still Alive centre. Kate Bouch is in charge of this operation and her post is paid for by the Girls Friendly Society – two-thirds, and by the Diocese – one-third. The premises they have leased are now almost ready to enable the mums and toddlers facilities to be provided with the downstairs front area being made into a nearly new shop. A knitting machine has been provided and they have the services of a person who is proficient with this type of machine.

Our next stop took in the basement community arts workshop with good facilities including a splendidly equipped dark room. The equipment here has been obtained from someone in the Diocese who became allergic to the chemicals and he sold it to D.V.V. at a knock-down price.

Our final call was to the Sight and Sound Music Workshop and S.O.S. Contact Centre. Here we met a group of young people who were directly involved with the music and the contact centre.'

The Fund has made a grant of £30,000 over three years towards the salary of the Project Co-ordinator and the Venture is also supported by the National Westminster Bank.

The Denaby Main Miners' Memorial Chapel, Sheffield

In the same area the Fund has provided £4,500 towards the construction of a Miners' Memorial Chapel.

Denaby is a very close knit community founded entirely on mining. Both local pits have closed and the village now has 'no reason for existing'. There is high unemployment both in the village of Denaby itself, and in the surrounding area of the Dearne Valley. The loss of job opportunities for young people and the loss of identity for the community as a whole are major problems.

In July 1987 work began on the Denaby Main Miners' Chapel. This is being built as an extension to the parish church and will form a unified church complex. The Chapel is being built as a 'permanent memorial to all miners who had worked the pits from the very first'.

The Holy Table, made of pit prop timber, balances on four Dowty props, normally used as roof supports underground. Behind, there is a cross cut of coal. British Coal's scientific department had to experiment to see how best to make the cross.

The Chapel is to be used for worship, prayer and quiet. Couples will have the opportunity to be married there. The Chapel and church complex will have the potential to meet the needs of the less mobile in the community. It will also have a cultural and educational purpose, not only for Denaby but also for the much wider area of South Yorkshire. The church complex will be suitable for conferences centred on the Chapel.

The Chapel was consecrated by the Bishop of Sheffield on Easter Sunday 1989.

St Mark's, Millfield, Sunderland

Millfield is in Sunderland, immediately south of the River Wear and inland of the town centre. The housing is Victorian, typically one or two-bedroomed single storey cottages which are either privately rented or owner occupied.

The style of the housing to a large extent determines the population. Small houses are ideal for first time buyers or for the elderly, but are more difficult for growing families, so the more materially successful middle-aged have moved from the parish, leaving a population which is biased towards each end of the age spectrum.

In common with the whole town of Sunderland, there is widespread unemployment in the parish with pockets of more than 20 per cent. This situation will certainly deteriorate if, as seems likely, the yards on the Wear are either reduced in size or closed. 32 per cent of those in employment in the ward which includes the parish are employed in 'manufacturing' – almost exclusively the shipyards. Despite the efforts of local council, provision of social facilities is very limited.

Violet Turpin from Millfield spoke at the Coventry service for the Church Urban Fund:

'The forces that rule our lives seem so big, the decisions are made so far from us.

Our shipyards were closed, all of them, did anybody really hear our cries of pain?

64

Sunderland has seen the loss of thousands of jobs with the closure of its shipyards over the past decade.

The lives of ordinary, decent people are changed by things that happen hundreds of miles away. It always seems to be the same, the damage comes from far away, the love comes from our own community.

Why can't the decision makers hear our voices?'

Saint Mark's Church, together with others sought to meet community needs in 1983 by the refurbishment of a large hall adjacent to the church. This was owned by the church, but had been dilapidated for many years. A large grant (£75,000) was applied for and obtained from the Urban Programme. The Hall was repaired using labour employed under the Community Programme. The first phase of this work was completed in January 1988, the second phase, the rebuilding of an old corrugated iron shed, in December 1988.

The new community use started in March 1988. The intention was to try to meet the needs of three sections of the community – the young people, the unemployed, and the elderly. Eventually work with these three groups will intermingle in the Hall, the craftroom and the ancillary rooms. Lack of funds has, of course, made it necessary to proceed cautiously with these activities, and work with the unemployed will be delayed until the structural work on the second phase is completed and the money is raised for equipping it.

The activities which have been started since phase I was opened in March have, of necessity, been self-financing. Groups with formal meeting times can ask for regular subscriptions from members. Those which are at present running include: Karate, Keep Fit, Altzhiemer's Disease Society Day Care, Kids' Club (for children 5–8), Kids' Club (for children 8–11), Church based youth activities (Pathfinders and Explorers), Over 60s (together with a lunch provision especially for the elderly infirm), mother and toddler club.

The workshop facilities will provide a unique feature in the town. The provision of workspace and tools will allow the middle-aged unemployed person to use and share his or her skill away from home and thus provide some of the benefits which previously have been provided by paid employment – self respect, companionship, a time structure. This formula has been well tried by, among others, the Impasse organisation in Middlesbrough. Because the workshop has a connecting door with the coffee bar, it is hoped that the 'magnet' of the workshop will also add to the casual use of the coffee bar.

The difficulty of managing the project as activity increases is a constraint on growth. For this reason plans for the future include the employment of a paid co-ordinator/manager, so the Church Urban Fund has agreed to make a grant of £22,000 over three years towards the staffing costs estimated at £8,400 p.a.

St Peter's, Huddersfield

In recent years the parish of St Peter's Huddersfield has embarked on a programme of restoring the church's fabric. This work has been undertaken in the context of discovering the parish's role and purpose and mission in an urban priority area.

In addition to the restoration of the fabric, the church embarked on the development of the church's crypt under the M.S.C.'s Community Programme. A community centre opened in the crypt in the spring of 1985 and became a major aspect of the church's work with the community. The activities centre on a coffee bar and canteen – these offer the opportunities of real change.

Stan Evans, Director of the Bishop's Centenary Fund in Wakefield, wrote in September 1989:

'Some weeks ago I visited the Church Urban Fund project beneath Huddersfield Parish Church. I had the story related to me of a young girl who had come to that project heavily addicted to drugs, and to buy those drugs had had to resort to prostitution. She was listened to and she was given the chance of a new life. She has recently secured a job in a local bank and she now can dream of a future.'

With the demise of the Community Programme the project has suffered the loss of its senior workers and project workers, but the Parochial Church Council is determined to continue its work of care and compassion in the community. The congregation is drawn on from all parts of Huddersfield and sees its mission in terms of outreach and care and compassion.

The change from the Community Programme to the Employment Training Scheme requires all trainees to have 40 per cent of their time in directed training. When the development of the Crypt took place in 1983–4, half of the Crypt was opened up. There is no possibility of doing any directed training in the open area of the Crypt, which is available to all members of the public at any time

Extending St Peter's Huddersfield into the community, December 1989.

when the Crypt is open. It is therefore proposed to develop the other half of the Crypt to enable the directed training to be held on the same site and so fulfil the requirements of the Employment Training Scheme.

UCANDUIT, Newcastle

UCANDUIT could have been 'done for' when the annual £75,000 M.S.C. grant stopped abruptly. But the centre Toc H founded in Elswick, Newcastle-upon-Tyne, five years ago to help the unemployed and those lacking the skills to cope with life, put its energies into survival and looked for other sources of funding . . . and got them.

Now, with adequate financial support and new, well equipped premises UCANDUIT is making a fresh start.

It is a smaller, leaner, organisation, catering for half the numbers it did before, but the quality of help it offers is, if anything, higher. It used to operate with five full-time staff and ten sessional tutors, with 730 people passing through the project annually. Now with just three full time staff, it will still offer training to between 350 and 400 people.

Development manager Keith Crocker, commented:

'This is a re-launch of UCANDUIT. We offer training in computer literacy and woodwork but we are very flexible and have a rolling clientele of between 35 or 40 people a week. The woodworking side is being run as a business, something we were unable to do before because of the way we were funded, and we try to give real jobs to people who may have been unemployed for so long they have lost confidence in themselves.

A number of good things came out of the change in circumstances. We have better premises, and we were very lucky to get them. From here we can operate on a commercial basis and that can only be of help to the sort of people we have coming here. Some of them may have been out of work for several years and have started to question whether they could cope with work again. Here they can rediscover what they are capable of.'

The Church Urban Fund has put £25,000 towards staff and running costs.

7

Community Care and Self-help

Pear Tree Craft Centre, Derby

1987 was the International Year of Shelter for the Homeless. In October 1985 the Social Responsibility Committee of the Baptist Churches in the East Midlands began to look at ways in which it could respond.

In February it initiated discussion between Pear Tree Baptist Church in Derby and the Padley Day Centre based in the city. The Padley is an ecumenically run centre which offers drop-in facilities for homeless people in Derby. Pear Tree Baptist Church is a multi-racial church in the inner city. Out of the discussions evolved the concept of a craft centre based on the church premises as an extension of the work of the Padley Day Centre.

Many of the people who meet in the Padley Day Centre are not homeless in the sense that they do not have a roof over their head, but they often live in very poor lodging or bed-sit accommodation. Pear Tree is a district in Derby where this sort of accommodation is found. These living conditions usually fail to provide the facilities and freedom that most people would come to expect from anything which could be called 'a home'. The Pear Tree Craft Centre provides space and freedom for people to develop and use their skills and explore their hobbies – the sort of things that most of us would do in our garage, lounge, kitchen or garden.

A Derbyshire County Council Grant of £42,000 provided the resource to convert, refurbish and equip the church hall. There is a large workshop area for woodwork and pottery, a studio for lighter crafts, a meeting and reading room, a dark-room for photography, an office, a kitchen and dining area. The centre was opened on 14 July 1988 when 200 people shared in a service of dedication. A Baptist minister led the service, the Bishop preached, a member of the Padley Day Centre unlocked the door, a county councillor unveiled the plaque and a Catholic priest blessed it.

All they needed was people, and they came. Richard is 36, has a speech impediment and, until a year ago, lived in a local psychiatric hospital. He was discharged into the community and the hospital authorities lost touch with him. His neighbours alerted the hospital to his plight; he was living in a hovel, had no food or amenities or money to buy anything. He visited his family and they gave him meals, unaware that these were the only times he ate. Intelligent though he is, he has a communication problem and he doesn't like to make a fuss. The Social Services found him a decent house, sorted him out financially and then referred him to the Pear Tree Craft Centre.

Peter is 24, also an ex-psychiatric patient, who received treatment for violent fits. His mother died two years ago – the last remaining member of his family. He visited the Padley Day Centre and they helped him get a council flat. All seemed well. A month later, he turned up at their door, about to be thrown out of his flat due to financial difficulties. Why hadn't he come before now? He felt ashamed at letting them down after all their help. The Padley Centre negotiated with the council a system for Peter to pay back the arrears. They also referred him to the Pear Tree Craft Centre.

Richard and Peter hit it off with each other straight away. Some at the Centre have difficulties understanding Richard's speech, yet Peter doesn't. Both enjoy woodwork and have been making bird-nesting boxes to sell for the centre.

The Centre manager is Bob Hollings, himself a former victim of the problems of the area. He was first of all helped by the local

Rug pegging at the Peartree Craft Centre, Derby.

Anglican Church where he became part-time verger. He is now full-time at Pear Tree, responsible for the development of its work.

Activities in this busy, crowded and exceptionally happy Centre are many.

There is a woodwork section, with good tools and proper workbenches where newcomers are started on making, amongst other things, wooden stools from a kit, including varnishing the finished products ready for sale. Furniture restoration work is carried out and all the helpers say that the important thing is to give the users tasks which they can accomplish, which will not bore them, but which will give them variety.

There is no shortage of volunteers, who come from local Churches. They blend in so well with the users that it is hard to distinguish one from the other.

The building itself is light and airy. Cheerful colours like bright greens and reds are used rather than the drabber institutional colours familiar to many of the users. The pear tree which gave the area its name is in the grounds next door, with a preservation order on it.

The Centre has been loaned a wheel, together with expensive tools, so a pottery workshop has been set up. This is one of the many ways in which the Centre has built up a good relationship with Pastures hospital, one of two local psychiatric hospitals which are helping the Centre to provide the kind of care in the community for discharged patients which is often lacking, although desperately needed.

The pottery has moulds for making Isle of Lewis chess pieces, provided by the hospital's Industrial Training Unit, some of whose technical instructors and helpers are 'on loan' as teachers. As with hospital I.T.U.s, the amount of money the users can earn from turning out goods for sale has to be limited to avoid their benefits being cut.

There is a dark room, set up with help from a local community arts project, and a quiet room for relaxation. It is intended that it will also be used by disabled people for whom a number of ideas are being canvassed, including sewing moccasins, a simple job that can help to build self-confidence since the finished product takes very little time.

The well equipped kitchen can serve meals to about 24 people a day – the only limitation really is on the seating area. They pay 50p for a main meal and a sweet including 'Jessie's special'. Jessie is one of the volunteers. Jessie is 80 and has only learned to cook over the last five years since her sister died. Now she quite happily makes quiches and pizzas, chocolate sponge puddings and sausage rolls for the centre – as well as simpler things like bangers and mash.

Her example is useful to the users: cookery is seen as part of the life skills that so many of them lack because they have been institutionalised and are then discharged with very few community facilities available to them.

After lunch there is an opportunity to sit down in the small lounge and share in prayers, a Bible reading and songs.

The Revd James Grote is secretary for Social Responsibility for Baptist churches in the East Midlands. He says the project is also economic, and it is working in partnership with government organisations, through the health authority, in trying to meet the needs of people in the immediate locality. James says the project is the church doing something that is not being done elsewhere.

What makes it different, says Grote, is that it is based on a philosophy of people's physical, emotional and spiritual needs. He says there is quite an emphasis 'on the fact that this has got something to do with our theology and what we believe as Christian people'. He sees prayer and worship as being an important ingredient of the workshop: 'We want to be sitting down from time to time to think about our understanding of the Kingdom and of salvation – it is terribly easy to do this sort of thing and not to let it affect your understanding of the Christian faith or without trying to work through your theology of social care.

'Why the Church? We always have to be careful that we pick up the bits that society won't. But part of the obligation for the church is to create a caring society, and not do the caring themselves.'

The Church Urban Fund has awarded £21,000 over three years towards Bob's salary and now the British Council of Churches have made Opportunities for Volunteers money available for an assistant who will co-ordinate projects.

Hutson Street Neighbourhood Project, Bradford

This area of Bradford is mainly inner-city residential with a population of about 19,000, 50 per cent of which is divided between those of Pakistani and Muslim origin, Bangladeshi or Indian or Afro-Caribbean in origin. Almost 25 per cent of the workforce is unemployed and the area has one of the highest number of semi-skilled and unskilled workers in the entire Bradford Metropolitan area.

The Hutson Street neighbourhood has been singled out as having a very high priority of need by the local Housing Authority because there is an abnormally high rate of turnover of tenants in the flats which make up much of the area. The Health Service is concerned because they see that there are severe health care problems, both for the elderly and the young. The local Social Services department regard the area as having severe 'communal deprivation' and have appointed two part-time community workers to the area. Two local churches in their audits have highlighted the considerable communal needs.

The Hutson Street Project is a joint initiative between the local churches and the local authority Social Services department. It aims to bring together groups and individuals in the area to give them a chance to carry out their own ideas for improving their quality of life. The project is housed in a converted launderette in a rather run-down shopping parade near the city centre. Pat Healy visited Hutson Street Project for the Fund, and wrote this very graphic account of what she saw and of the people she met.

'I visited on the craft afternoon and the first thing that hits you is the noise and chaos as more than a dozen adults and a similar number of children crowd into the small space – it used to be a launderette. On this occasion, all the adults are women although some male parents come sometimes.

'Two groups were working on ideas for a mural which is to be the project's signature on the outside of the building. One group is using the floor, the only space left, another tries to use the table. They have already painted two ideas for it – a child skipping, and washing leading to a rainbow, recalling the present and past of the place.

'Jenny from the local Community Arts project is helping. She asks the women to look for more ideas for the mural to bring next time – family photographs, snaps of places they have visited, magazine pictures – anything they feel expresses the feeling of the place. The idea immediately sparks off the women who can think of a lot of suitable things they have at home. Jenny wants to use tiny Italian mosaics for the mural – expensive but "cheerful and bright and it lasts forever" unlike the broken crockery sometimes used for similar signs.

'The noticeboard lists an invitation to join a local artists and cartoonists club (no experience needed); an indoor market and white elephant stall; an exhibition on the lives of Asian women in Britain.

'There's also a trip to the Blackpool illuminations at £2 for adults and 50p for children over three – sold out with more than 100 people signed up. Trips are an important part of the life of the project – it can organise a trip for £2 a family instead of the £20 it would cost to do on their own, which locals could not afford. The project asked for £1,500 from Children in Need for summer activities and got it. That paid for six trips, and there's money left over so it is now to be used for autumn and Christmas activities.

'The trips "broke up the summer" and gave people something to do according to Christine, aged 38, who is proudly cuddling her granddaughter, Ainsley, aged 7 months, while Ainsley's mum Sharon, aged 17, plays with Christine's youngest son (and Sharon's younger brother) Matthew, aged 16 months – all regulars at the project.

'One of the trips was to Morecambe where they managed to get free passes to the funfair. Elaine Appelbee says "It is really important that the adults have a good time as well as the children."

'Christine is by no means the oldest woman there: Kathleen is 62, and in charge of her granddaughter, Tanya aged 3, while Audrey is 66. The women make it clear that they enjoy mixing across the age groups; indeed they scarcely notice it any more. Most of them have been coming since the start in May, and give a variety of reasons like "nowhere else to go", "It gets me out of home", "I've made new friends". "It gets me out of bed," says an exhausted woman who adds "my daughter won't go to bed before five o'clock in the morning".

'They like coming because "We're like a family – we go to each other with problems, that's what we are here for – to help people in trouble." They are proud of their special groups where "we decide what trips we are going on." They think men don't come much because they prefer to socialise in the pub.

'The women have organised a jumble sale in the last week and raised £180 – and gave £60 to Bangladesh. They are already thinking of organising something for Pancake day and possibly an Easter Parade next year. These are women whom Elaine describes as "voiceless, choiceless and powerless" with absolutely nothing materially and whose potential has been locked up inside them.

'There is a prayer half-hour once a week, and a poster advertising it asks "is there anything special you would like us to pray for? It is the time when we will pray for anything connected with the centre and the people. YOU ARE WELCOME TO JOIN IN." This week's activities: Monday a.m. – playgroup for over threes; p.m.

mother & toddler group. Tuesday p.m. – friendship group. Wednesday a.m. – centre specials; p.m. – craft class. Thursday a.m. – training on opening the building; p.m. – welfare rights and playgroup. Friday a.m. – playgroup; p.m. – open session.

'The Thursday morning training is being provided because people wanted the centre to open on Friday afternoons. So they are being trained on welcoming people when they arrive, creating a relaxed atmosphere and the more mundane tasks of ensuring things are locked up and so on. It will make it a "building opened by and for the people" says Elaine.

'Elaine is employed by the Mothers' Union, and works with Ginny Murphy and Chris Rollings, both social services employees. The three women between them work the equivalent of one full-time post at the project.

'Elaine says when she talks to groups in other places, church goers say they give clothes "and I say that is good, but not good enough. As Christians, we have to ask why they need to be giving clothes."

'Elaine and Ginny say they are having to create a community artificially and have knocked personally on all doors to try and do that. What they are doing works because of the approach, says Elaine.

' "Instead of approaching people from a problem base, we go in and make friends with people and what we are interested, in our approach to them, is that they are independent, creative people with potential. They know the situation they are facing, they know what will improve their quality of life and their children's quality of life. All the ideas in this project have come from them."

'There were no activities for the first few weeks, and then the women came up with a list of ideas which they organised with support from the workers. Ginny points out that the women may not have been able to put into precise words what they wanted, but their meaning was clear. They suggested a group for all ages, for example, and that became the friendship group which organises things like trips to museums.

'Both Elaine and Ginny were amazed at the women's achievement in organising the jumble sale – which turned into something much bigger, once they began to discuss what they wanted to do. Elaine, worrying that they are trying to take on too much, found herself gently patronised by women who a few months before would have felt themselves capable of anything.

'The project is turning them into the reverse of being "voiceless, choiceless and powerless". Elaine points to simple things, like longing for coffee but not being able to afford it, but realising "if we bring people together, if we all put 10p in we can all have coffee – they can begin to come together and have a choice." In the same way, by voicing the needs in their lives and coming up with a number of ideas they begin to have a voice over their lives, and power to do something about their needs. Ginny sums it up as "confidence building".

'They pay £10 a year rent for the shop, a housing department property, and it cost £16,000 to refurbish. There are 53 adults using the place regularly and about the same number of kids; 25 to 30 come at least once a week. They want to move to larger premises which the housing department is willing to provide, but there are financial problems. Equipment for the present project was to come from Urban Aid, but they have just heard that it has been refused.'

The Church Urban Fund has made a grant of £10,930 over four years to help with the renovation of the launderette, and with support for the workers.

Communicare: Sheffield

Communicare, a group rehabilitation project is based in half of the church of St Mary's, Bramall Lane, in the centre of Sheffield. The area is one of Victorian terraced streets and has a high proportion of Asian inhabitants.

All participants in Communicare are unemployed. Many of them have additional difficulties, often connected with unemployment, breakdowns and marital disruptions. The rest of the group have less spectacular needs, and are usually seeking work experience or basic training.

This mixture of people with different kinds of need is deliberate, and is a fundamental part of the way that the scheme operates. Distinctions are intentionally blurred, and all participants are treated on the same footing, whether they are referred by social workers or from hospitals, or are just unemployed and seeking work, or are in the group as voluntary helpers.

All participants in the scheme are referred to as 'volunteers'. The term originated with the scheme's beginnings in the Voluntary Projects Programme, and has been deliberately retained as a way of avoiding 'labelling' within a very mixed group.

The volunteers undertake various sorts of work. A visiting and gardening service gives practical help to local elderly and housebound people. They print and distribute their own community magazine, and print and collate many other magazines and leaflets. The print room provides a regular service for Barnardo's, for the Blood Transfusion Service, and for South Yorkshire Police. The volunteers gain experience working in a group, they have access to training in print work and they are encouraged to improve their basic skills, and if possible move, into employment.

Each volunteer is individually assessed, counselled and guided during his or her stay in the scheme. They are all encouraged to progress and to participate in the various sorts of activities available. The scheme gives participants an opportunity to recover and grow in a mixed, accepting group with a common purpose.

Finishing a print job, Communicare, Sheffield.

Dr Chris Knight, Project Manager of Communicare, says,

'We see participants arrive who are so beaten down by their experiences that they find any form of social contact difficult. For some, even talking without the group is a large step forward, and joining in the easy repetitive work of collating magazines is an achievement. We see participants recover their self respect and their motivation. About one-third eventually go on into employment, more than half of these into the Community Programme, but a substantial number into 'real' jobs – a surprisingly large proportion, given the nature of the group and the continuing difficulty of finding any work in Sheffield.'

In the past, Communicare has relied on funding from the M.S.C.'s Voluntary Projects Programme for the four staff and overheads. Communicare is now seeking independent funding from March 1989, because the flexibility of Communicare in moving participants on from one sort of activity or training to another, could not be accommodated within the Employment Training framework. Some income will be earned by the print room, but support is needed to enable the project to reorganise its work and to develop. The Fund has made a grant to Communicare of £30,000 towards their running costs for three years.

The Star Centre, Gosforth, Newcastle

It is said the best cup of tea in Gosforth is served by Billy Atkinson in the Star Centre drop-in where the beverage has been known to give new hope to people, as well as quenching thirst. Star Centre Ltd was started nearly two years ago by priests of many denominations alongside the local Jewish Community as a means of helping the unemployed and poor in the Fawdon, North Kenton and Gosforth areas of Newcastle upon Tyne.

There had been plenty of talk but little action until the old Coxlodge School in Jubilee Road came on to the property market.

Church leaders in the area banded together to lease the building and open it up to a number of activities, contributing towards the life of the community.

Patrick Cotton, Team Rector of the Parish of the Epiphany and St Mary's, Fawdon, recalls that negotiations took place with the unemployed very much in mind. He said: 'It was a way of establishing a place of contact. I used to notice when I visited people there was nothing I could do for them or offer them. Now there is the Star Centre. People who may not find it easy to walk into a church have no qualms about walking into the centre.'

Volunteers cleaned and decorated the building which had been used as a builder's store. Space was let to a variety of organisations, among them the Sanderson Hospital charity shop, a job club, and the Shaw project which provides sheltered housing and work training for people with special needs. A pensioners' group, the Starlets, based itself in the building, and the Baptist church took a room for services and meetings.

'All these things were within our remit and the organisations that moved in welcomed us as we welcomed them,' said Revd Cotton. 'We could offer accommodation which they had found hard to come by.'

With the help of the Church Urban Fund and the British Council of Churches, the managers of the Star Centre hired a development worker, Linda Hinton, and a volunteer organiser, Dorothy Moore. Linda has her salary paid by the Northern Rock Building Society, while Dorothy is sponsored by the Department of Social Security.

They have pitched into the task of setting up worthwhile community projects and getting local people to help them.

The drop-in café and the charity shop attract most people to the centre. The café could probably do better with more equipment and additional volunteer workers.

The man who runs it, former bus driver Billy Atkinson said: 'We do teas, coffees and snacks. We can do bacon, sausage and chips and we know that it is the main meal of the day for a few. If we were not here they might not eat at all. They would not go out to shop.' Billy's wife, Margaret, helps him and says they could do more if they had a better cooker and a few more volunteer helpers.

Linda Hinton said: 'It provides a place for people to meet and talk most days of the week. It is offering the community something, but we could offer much more if we had a little money. We are always struggling for cash.'

She hopes to get the Citizens Advice Bureau to hold sessions on the premises for a couple of hours a week, and wants to open a second hand furniture store for youngsters who are setting up home for the first time.

She is also exploring the possibility of setting up a Credit Union. 'We have plenty of ideas, what we need is a little bit of funding as seed corn,' she said.

The Fund has made a grant of £36,450 over three years which will help to explore further possibilities for use of the building and to help consolidate the project.

St Philips, Nelson, Blackburn

The town of Nelson prospered with the establishment of the cotton mills and grew rapidly with the building of large numbers of terraced cottages to house the large labour force. But many of the mills have now closed and unemployment is steadily rising, made worse by the closure in recent years of two of the town's other major employers, Victory V Sweets and Smith & Nephew Textiles.

The neat terraced streets of this cotton town owe much to a long tradition of civic pride. But behind the facades live scores of lonely old people and depressed young families, whose hopelessness leaves them without the energy to accept the large local Asian community.

Rosemary and Stewart Hartley with the plans for St Philip's, Nelson.

The Revd Stewart Hartley, priest in charge of St Philip's Church, was born in Nelson and knew the problems when he was asked to take on the parish five years ago. He came prepared to make the Church 'a serving church – a Church that cared and reached out'.

That has been partly achieved by Stewart, and Rosemary his wife, living on the council estate; their home has become an informal drop-in centre for local people, whose needs have drawn them into the Church.

But his original plan to replace the forbidding, enormous church seating over 800 people, with a smaller one and a community centre was rejected. But the old church has been renovated at a cost of £32,000, a sum raised by the parish, and will be partly converted to provide community facilities.

A Church Urban Fund grant will finance a community worker to run a project, building on the work Stewart has begun. Three groups need help; young families, elderly people and the ethnic minority, particularly Asian mothers. A grant of £43,150 has been made.

For families, there will be a mother and toddler group, where children can be cared for while their mothers have someone to talk to, particularly about their child rearing problems. Rosemary says that is needed because most young mothers were 'dragged up' like their own mothers, who had no experience of good parenting to pass on. So breast feeding is virtually non-existent, and the idea that children should be put to bed is a foreign concept. Bewildered mothers do not understand why their children are fractious when awake.

Hopes of better things are squashed by fathers whose ambitions for their daughters stop at a 'job' on the Y.T.S. scheme or at the mill. Years of neglect and the 'oppression of three generations of working at the mills' cannot be easily overcome by professionals like health visitors.

But the support Rosemary and Stewart give raises hope. For example, Alan and Wendy Heap are coping with the loss of Alan's job at Victory V, but he is dismayed that the factory is being pulled down. He says: 'They could have turned it into a heritage museum – it has been there for 120 years. It isn't the jobs – it is the memory. It is part of my life.'

Alan's new confidence makes him thoughtful, too, about how the project can improve things: 'It is a good thing for the Church to do. It could be good for getting Asians and whites together so we can get on better.'

For old people, there will be a drop-in centre. The need is shown by Peggy Ashcroft who spends her day-off from work visiting elderly people. Many are housebound widows, Stewart has 60 funerals a year. Peggy says she mainly listens as lonely old people pour out their problems which they dwell on because they are on their own a lot.

Stewart hopes old people will feel free to come to the centre and stay as long as they want, have a meal if they choose to, and have somebody with time to sit and chat. Gladys Turner, a spirited but housebound 84 year old, says she hopes it will be run like a centre she remembers from her married days in Derbyshire, with hot drinks at cost price, a cheap midday meal, and the over 60s raising money themselves for treats.

Gladys was always active but her disability now means she has to travel by ambulance to Church, Bible study groups, and a day centre. She is fed up being on her own at home and angry that the caring seems to have gone out of welfare.

Mischievously she suggests that old people are now 'surplus to requirements' so 'they ought to do them in at 80'. More seriously Gladys says that 'old age is no picnic' while insisting that she is 'one of the fortunate ones' because of her interest in the Church.

The needs of the ethnic minorities are not so well known, apart from the isolation of Asian women. It was the local Pentecostal Church that first welcomed them as worshippers. But the local

Children praying at the C of E St Philip's Aided Infant and Junior School, situated in the most deprived area of Nelson in Lancashire. Seventy-five per cent of the 135 children attending school are of an ethnic minority, but their parents still prefer to send them to a religious school even though it may not be of their denomination.

Church School, with 85 per cent Asian pupils, is making progress through a home/school liaison officer who is building links with the parents. Stewart hopes the Asian Christian Fellowship, which is keen to be part of the project, will run the planned playgroup for Asian children and a simple translation service for the Church for Asian women.

Faith in the City was a catalyst for the project. Stewart says the report saw the problems, including 'the sin of the Church in that it was complacent about it'. He adds:

'We have surrounding parishes which are rolling in money who have never once said "can we help?" It is not that they don't care – they have never realised, as *Faith in the City* did, that it is not a question of people being able to pull their own fingers out – that they need outside help.

Stewart hopes that local people 'will see in that building, instead of an irrelevance, a focus – somewhere they feel free to be part of the Church'. In his own house to house visiting he has found 'a wonderful good will towards the Church', combined with hurt, anger and puzzlement about why the Church has not done more.

The Church Urban Fund grant will make the difference between a 'ramshackle make do and mend affair' and being able to take on a community worker, stop worrying about the building, and get on with caring for the people.

The project will have to be self-supporting eventually. Stewart does not feel it is part of the vision that it would always be propped up, particularly when people usually on the receiving end want to be able to give.

Stewart believes the project is an attempt to meet the needs that no-one else can 'because the needs come to us'. But there are more important reasons for the Church taking the lead. 'If the Church is to have a vital, real witness it is to care for the poor. The mission of the church is to do that – to heal the sick, give to the poor, set free the captives, release the oppressed. That was Jesus' message and that must be the Church's message now.'

8

New Lives

It is always in the personal stories and tragedies of life that cries for help shout the loudest. When Jesus told the parable of the Good Samaritan, it was to emphasise the cry of need from one person to another, and to show how easy it is to find reasons for passing by on the other side.

Daybreak, Dagenham: A drug abuse centre

Daybreak began in 1985, created by the Revd Deryck Spratley, Vicar of Dagenham who buried three young people who had died from drug overdoses within a few months.

Believing that there is a Christian alternative to drug addiction, Daybreak offers a drugs service, counselling individuals and groups, as well as referring those who have a drug dependency problem to clinics and rehabilitation centres. It aims to help anyone contacting them about a drug problem, particularly young people involved or experimenting with drugs. They also offer support and counselling to families and friends of drug dependents. The bulk of the work is carried out on the streets, and in the houses and flats of their clients.

Daybreak's workers are funded by Urban Aid and are hopelessly overstretched. The Church Urban Fund is supporting the employment of a second worker who will liaise with professional and voluntary bodies directly involved with drugs, and also expand existing work with the children of drug abusers.

Mike Thorpe started his work among those abusing chemicals in 1972 at the age of 21, when he worked at Spitalfields Crypt, a Christian Centre for alcoholic vagrants in East London.

At the age of 23 he became Assistant Director of Life for the World Trust in London and spent some years living with youngsters who had chronic drug problems. He then moved on to Portsmouth and Scotland where he worked with disturbed youngsters. Throughout his career he has always kept in touch with drug addiction and its influence in society.

Mike now works in Dagenham as full-time Youth and Drug Liaison Officer at Daybreak.

Mike Thorpe, from Daybreak, Dagenham, talking with Brian.

Daybreak aims to send the users into therapy after arranging short term medication through their own G.P.s. 'There's no point in starting, says Mike, if you can't provide both short term medication and long term support. We do a lot of work in the community – visit them, assess their motivation to get therapy and build bridges with the local community.'

'Daybreak is offering them a Christian alternative,' says Mike. But, 'we believe for that to be effective we must also be practical'. The users need to change their life style and that means giving them an alternative. 'We do believe that through the Christian gospel there is an opportunity to give them a new purpose for living and a new foundation of that life.'

But something has to be put in the place of the 'chemicals' as Mike calls the drugs, and that is not easy when the chemicals change them morally, emotionally and socially. Only 5 per cent began using drugs for emotional reasons. For 95 per cent it was curiosity, pleasure, or peer group pressure – and then they became addicted.

Daybreak has dealt with 1,000 people so far, 200 users and their families. Mike says 'When they go into therapy we have to keep in constant touch with them.' They also deal with prison visits: it costs users £100–120 a day to 'keep themselves normal. It brings them into crime'. Maintaining someone's motivation to stop using drugs is a major problem. Motivation comes and goes.

'You constantly give them hope for tomorrow that they can stop. But it is very difficult to keep them motivated. You get them prepared and at the last moment they won't go. You constantly keep in touch with people – you don't drop them or put pressure on them. You befriend them. You remove the fear they have that you are going to take away their chemicals. Drug users have needs just like we have. Any person or organisation is a threat if they don't want to stop.'

Measuring success is difficult: when people stop, it is often only for a period of time and then they start again. Mike says that four out of five who completely come off go back within six months because most of their friends are on drugs. Like Brian, who Mike says has gone back to using quite heavily since he returned home from prison recently.

Brian looks like the young man in the government's anti-heroin T.V. advertisements: grey and shaking, and his voice is slurred. He says he wants to come off, but he is spending time with his old mates again. His parents are concerned, but anxious that his example may be copied by his two younger brothers. He insists they won't use 'because they have seen what it has done to me'.

Examples like that breed the idea that drugs programmes are not successful. Success for Daybreak is to bring someone to a changed life style without using chemicals. Letters from clients sometimes bring hope: Mike has just (September 1988) received a letter from a young woman now in a therapy unit in Shropshire.

She writes: 'My initial depression was almost too much to bear but I must say that my trip back to Barking has done me the power of good after all.

'The programme will *work* for me. I am NOT here just for court. I thought I was, but now I *know* it's for me.

'I am coping better, I am getting into my work, the projects are beginning to get off the ground now. But most important of all, I am really beginning to feel at home and I am happy too.'

But Mike says that it is very difficult when people who have been away on therapy come back to the same kind of environment. Dagenham has one of the biggest heroin problems in Britain; one that leads a number of grannies to remove their daughters' children and bring them up themselves to protect them.

That hasn't happened to Lorraine yet. She's 22, married with a three-year-old son Aaron and first heard about Daybreak seven months ago. She now comes one or two days a week. 'It makes you feel wanted,' she says.

Her husband, Terry, was using drugs when they met – he's now in prison for shoplifting to raise the money to support his habit.

Lorraine says she knows she is off drugs because she used her social security money this week to buy herself a pair of trousers instead of heroin. But Mike thinks she is 'dabbling' still. She has been on holiday to the Isle of Wight with Daybreak – 'it was nice' she says. But she didn't like camping very much, particularly when Mike was in a boarding house. But she adds 'everyone gets on with everyone else and it is just a nice big family'.

Deryck Spratley says he is pleased by the way the project is going, and by the fact that his congregation has been totally supportive. One result of the work is that lots of people Daybreak is not directly in touch with know about it.

The project exists on a shoestring. Deryck says it is hard to raise money, but he is 'grateful that we have a building like this'.

And he's very hopeful that the project will be picked up by the local council if necessary; the leader has told him 'our professionals have not been able to do much – maybe you with your extra commitment can'. Deryck stresses that 'It is our principal virtue that we are 100 per cent Christian motivated.'

The Church Urban Fund has made a grant of £27,000 over three years. This will help to pay for work with the children of drug abusers.

New Assembly of Churches, Rehabilitation and Aftercare Project

The National Black Clergy Consultative Group was formed as a result of a meeting of London Pastors of the Black-led churches. They had become aware of the frustration amongst young people, especially within the Caribbean community, and the anxiety shown by their parents and elders. The negative stereotyping of black youth has had an adverse effect, and the N.B.C.C.G. was impressed by the concern shown amongst the younger members within their own congregations.

The project which they began is to encourage offenders, ex-

Lavine Hudson, gospel singer and patron of the New Assembly
aftercare project, supporting Church Urban Fund week.

offenders and those at risk of offending, to come to terms with their
situation and to re-establish themselves in the community with
confidence and self-respect. Two hundred volunteers visit and
befriend offenders. In order to achieve maximum benefit from
their efforts, it became necessary to appoint a co-ordinator.

The Revd Carmel Jones has the task of bringing the work of the
London Churches together to form a unified approach.

These stories are typical:

Tom, a drug pusher and user, was on remand in Pentonville
awaiting trial for his fourth conviction. He requested help to
obtain an assessment on his suitability for rehabilitation from
a centre in Oxford. This was done by providing £70 towards
the £100 that was needed. The report was sent to the presiding
Judge who sent Tom to a Drug Rehabilitation Centre for four
months. He has now kicked the habit and no longer supplies
drugs.

AGE: 21   RELIGION: Anglican   LOCATION: Hackney

Danny was sentenced to nine months in prison for grievous
bodily harm. His family was befriended and he has now

completed his sentence and has so far kept himself out of trouble. He hopes to get a flat transfer out of the area.

AGE: 19   RELIGION: Anglican   LOCATION: Brixton

Roger was sentenced to six months in prison for mugging. He has completed his sentence and has been helped to find work.

AGE: 18   RELIGION: Pentecostal   LOCATION: Streatham

Tony was on remand for seven months on rape charges brought by his former girlfriend and was not happy with his solicitor. He was helped to get a change of solicitor and within seven weeks was on trial at the Old Bailey. He was acquitted of the charge and is now back with his employers who kept his job open for him.

AGE: 20   RELIGION: Methodist   LOCATION: Peckham

The Church Urban Fund is providing £50,000 over five years to help with the employment of a development officer working with young offenders who are seeking employment and who wish to start their own businesses. The project is also supported by Guinness.

St James with St Bede, Birkenhead

The parish of St James' with St Bede is set in the North End of Birkenhead. The parish extends from the now largely disused Birkenhead docks through a large local authority housing area up through a large area of smaller and terraced houses to a small 'middle class' housing area. The parish is mixed, but comprises a large area (over one half) of recognised deprivation, with unemployment in all age groups running at well over the national average.

The initial vision of the Revd Barrie Guage, the incumbent, was the establishment of a viable Christian congregation which would be able to reach out into the community with the Gospel. In 1984 this seemed a virtual impossibility with an elderly congregation totalling about twenty-five, depressed and lacking in any vision of growth. However, now it's very different: average congregations are 150–250 each Sunday with many potential and growing local leaders, all aware that growth has come about by prayer and proclamation.

In 1986 the staff expanded to include a Parish Evangelist, a Church Army Captain. Among his specific tasks was the seeking of a toehold into the surrounding community so the church could provide a front-line service of help and advice in the face of obvious need.

Opposite the church at that time was an Unemployed Resource Centre, set up by the local trade unions and funded by the Merseyside County Council. This was an advice and campaigning centre in its heyday with many paid employees. The demise of the County Council meant the immediate withdrawal of funding. By October 1986 the Centre was struggling.

The Roundabout Centre and St James' Church, Birkenhead.

A preliminary meeting with the leaders of the Centre led eventually to the founding of a partnership to run and finance the Centre. This partnership involves the original Resource Centre Group, St James' Church, Parents Against Drug Abuse (a local parent support group serving an area among the worst for drug addiction in the country), and BUS Books (a second hand bookshop set up by the original centre to raise money following the withdrawal of County Council funding).

On 1 October 1987 the Centre, now called the Roundabout Centre, was opened.

Ann Foster was seconded to the Centre by the Chester Board of Social Responsibility to work for one-and-half days per week.

Ann's role was that of a social worker dealing with a range of problems from the care of children, the needs of single parent families right through to the love and patience needed in dealing with the elderly. Ann was presented as the 'Centre's own social worker' emphasising that she was not part of the D.H.S.S. establishment since this would have seriously hampered her work in this area.

The need for a social worker is borne out by the testimony of the welfare rights workers who are currently dealing with over 50 visitors per day. They are able to deal with benefit problems, and are not able to help with many of the other issues raised. Parents Against Drug Abuse have also set up an office in the Centre. As St James' Church is involved in the project, there is a strong Christian influence and Ann's added abilities as a Christian to counsel, help and pray with and for people, has been invaluable.

Ann worked within a team of approximately 20 staff and volunteers. Relationships had been built up so that many now confided in her. The Diocese increased her hours so that she eventually worked four and a half days, but this commitment could not be continued by the Diocese beyond the end of 1988.

The number of visitors to the Centre has trebled and with the opening of a drop-in centre the need for a full-time social worker arrived. The work already generated requires also the work of an assistant.

The Church Urban Fund has made a grant of £20,000 over three years towards the salary of a Christian worker and social work assistant at the Roundabout. They will also help with counselling advice for families.

The Mustard Seed, Walsall

Doug Jones was one of the thousands of victims of the collapse of the industrial base of the West Midlands that made Walsall's epithet as 'the town of a hundred trades' ring hollow.

He was made redundant after thirteen years working for a local brewery. But his hobby as a motorbike racer proved his salvation: he had taught himself to repair and make spare parts for his own bikes – and that was the key to starting a new business.

He won the first business award of the Mustard Seed Group, started by members of the congregation of St Matthew's Church,

Walsall, in direct response to Faith in the City. His prize was £2,000, plus a free factory unit for a year given by Walsall District Council. The money bought an air plasma machine which cuts quickly and accurately the metal used for spare parts for classic motorbikes.

Doug says that people are now so proud of their irreplaceable classic Nortons that they will pay handsomely to restore them to their former glory – and then display them like ornaments in their living rooms. He is confident that the engineering skills he has taught himself will enable him to thrive even if the bottom drops out of the bike market.

His business is one of several the Mustard Seed group has helped get started – with financial help from the Church Commissioners, the Lichfield Diocese, a charitable trust, the local authority and the Government.

The Church Urban Fund is now contributing £8,357 over two years to help to pay the salary of the industrial promotions officer, Robert Snaith. The Mustard Seed group was the brainchild of the Revd Roger Sainsbury, the then Vicar of St Matthews. He arrived in Walsall just at the point when industry was collapsing. Walsall itself has lost 38,000 manufacturing jobs since 1971 and 1,000 firms closed in the region in the second quarter of 1986.

Mr Sainsbury knew about the effects of unemployment because he had previously worked in Canning Town in London and in Liverpool. But he was still unprepared for what he found in his parish.

'People were in a state of shock,' he says. 'The West Midlands had never expected unemployment. Everyone was affected – accountants, engineers and so on. It was not a question of lack of ability.'

He organised a group of engineers, accountants, industrialists, businessmen and trade unionists, all members of St Matthews, to meet the Bishop of Wolverhampton to discuss *Faith in the City*.

'We wanted to see if there was anything we could do to respond. It was a mixture of people with power and the powerless,' Mr Sainsbury says. 'We felt very small and powerless ourselves, but we believed something could be done. We felt, as Christians, that if we prayed God would guide us.'

The group was called 'Mustard Seed' in the hope that something very small might lead to something big. Mr Sainsbury was surprised at the enthusiasm generated. The group knew that Walsall was regarded as a high risk area but decided to seek investment nevertheless. They invited to Walsall the Church Commissioners, and then the Dean of St Pauls who had gathered together a group of City businessmen who were themselves looking for a way to respond to *Faith in the City*.

Walsall Council hosted both visits, these resulted in the Church Commissioners investing £250,000 in new business starter units for which the Prince of Wales laid the foundation stone in 1987, and plans for a housing and cottage industry development as well as conversion of a church for community use from the Dean of St Pauls' group.

Mr Snaith, a committed Christian, with twenty-seven years experience in business, banking and industry, started work as the new industrial promotions officer. He says many people try to start up businesses with little idea about raising capital, finding premises and the kind of venture that will work. He persuaded one man who wanted to set up as a painter and decorator instead to use his £800 worth of photographic equipment to turn his hobby into a new business. Other possible businesses include a dance school in Darlaston that two experienced women teachers want to open, an Asian jewellery shop, and a West Indian accessory and cosmetic business that two sisters want to start.

Those are in line with the town's year's business award scheme. In the first year all 18 applicants for the award were white men; now a special effort is being made to encourage women and people from the ethnic community to apply. Unfortunately, although the prize money will start at £2,000, this time the scheme cannot offer free factory units.

Mr Sainsbury said that it was slow work but the group's initial faith was justified by what is beginning to happen. He says the Fund's support should give continuity to Mr Snaith's work and help to show people who have given that the Church is committed to this sort of activity. He hopes that the grant will lead to Mr Snaith's appointment being stretched from the original two years to ten 'because there is a job of work to be done for the next ten years'.

Now, Roger Sainsbury has moved on to new work and Beryl Metcalf, the projects officer, said the group is reviewing its task through prayer and brain storming.

'We will still concentrate on the problems of the unemployed,' she said. 'The whole project was created by the last vicar of St Matthews and the church got involved because people felt that unemployment is such an evil in our society. Levels were very high round here – 25 per cent and higher in some parts. It had such a bad effect on people.

'It is part of the Kingdom. One should try and reduce unemployment. Just as Jesus fed the hungry because they needed it, so today people need jobs and we should try and generate them.'

9

Community and Race Relations

One of the most important and most sensitive areas of work for those in all local communities, is how they approach the arrival of newcomers. If people are from overseas then the problems of integration, of understanding a different faith, culture and set of traditions can be very great. It is those who live in the inner-city areas who first have to work through these questions. The East End of London has seen waves of immigrants arrive and pass through for almost all of the last 500 years. Experience in Liverpool has been similar. Over the past forty years there have come generations of people, now permanently settled in England, from Commonwealth countries and beyond.

The Fund supports many projects where issues of immigration and race are prominent. Questions of colour, racism and prejudice on the part of many people in England are not very far from the surface. These will not be resolved easily. If they have the will, Churches can play a great part in breaking down prejudice. Because they are 'on the ground' in every part of England they can have a unique understanding of local situations and, with others, play their part in building up understanding and better community relations.

Within immigrant communities there are particular areas of difficulty and frustration. Lord Scarman, in his report on the Brixton riots, spoke of the position of young people:

'Many of the young people of Brixton are therefore born and raised in insecure social and economic conditions and in an impoverished physical environment. They share the desires and expectations which our materialist society encourages. At the same time, many of them fail to achieve educational success and on leaving school face the stark prospect of unemployment. Many of these difficulties face white as well as black youngsters, but it is clear that they bear particularly heavy on young blacks. In addition, young black people face the burden of discrimination, much of it hidden and some of it

95

unconscious and unintended . . . it would be surprising if they did not feel a sense of frustration and deprivation. And living much of their lives on the streets, they are brought into contact with the police who appear to them as the visible symbols of the authority of society which has failed to bring them its benefits or do them justice.'

Community workers and many in the Churches are still voicing the same feelings as those of Lord Scarman.

Some projects in the chapters of this book are created by black people for black people. Others are projects designed specifically to assist black people settle into a wider local community. Other projects arise from an attempt by a church to bring together different groups within a community.

St James Handsworth, Birmingham

St James was built in 1839 to serve the thousands who came to work in Handsworth's growing industries. In the late eighteenth century, Boulton & Watt set up the first ever mass production of steam engines at their Soho Foundry and so effectively powered the Industrial Revolution throughout the world.

Local ancillary industries quickly grew in a huge variety of trades. Because of its green spaces and fresh air Handsworth also rapidly became a desirable home for the managers and clerks of booming Birmingham.

The churches flourished. Even in the 1930s, when St James held over 1,100, late-comers for Matins would not find a seat. After 1945, much began to change. The rows of Victorian terraces began to show their age. People moved away and Handsworth's new residents, from the Caribbean and the Punjab as well as from the British Isles, came in large numbers. Here they could find cheap available housing for purchase or rent.

Change in the mainstream churches was slow. Chapels and Free Churches closed, many selling their buildings to new, largely black, churches, or to people of other faiths. Those remaining shrank in confidence and numbers.

As an interregnum began in September 1982, Bishop Montefiore, then Bishop of Birmingham, visited and was blunt. 'This Victorian monstrosity must come down!' he told the P.C.C. He certainly had a point. The building, though beautiful within, is a little strange to look at from the outside.

But Bishop Hugh had underestimated the faith and determination of the congregation. Faced with closure, many, particularly among the oldest and longest standing, grasped that St James would either change or die. And if it was to remain, then it must be used fully and be truly the parish's church.

The Revd Rob Morris was appointed Priest in Charge in May 1983 with a brief from the Bishop to work with the congregation and the parish through whatever change was right.

The present St James, Handsworth, is set among some of the most severe inner city deprivation in Birmingham. It has a population of 16,000 which is currently very mixed, comprised of Asians, mostly Sikhs, but with a significant number of Christians, Afro-Caribbeans, Vietnamese, Moslems from Bangladesh and an ageing and impoverished white population. The problems of unemployment are acute – over 40 per cent – and the incidence of bad housing and family stress is high. Half the population is under 25.

75 per cent of the houses are owner-occupied but half of these are decaying rapidly with owners too poor to repair them. The parish has many fragmented families and broken homes yet much informal neighbourly caring. The area is depressed, yet the churches and temples within it vigorous and innovative.

St James seeks to improve its considerable investment in the local community by re-ordering its large church to make it serve the community's current needs. It is spending £190,000 to provide facilities within the church building for use by a number of voluntary community projects:

Basera Project – for elderly Asian people. This will provide midday meals, recreation, craft and learning facilities and also care for the pre-school children often left all day with their grandparents whilst their parents are working.

Inter-church endeavour – a Handsworth base for work with young unemployed people.

The Holyhead Association for Community Help – a family-based project seeking to offer child care support for elderly Asians and training, counselling and workshops for young mothers on benefit who have at present no way out of the poverty trap.

The parish church has a hand in other enterprising projects, notably through the community ministry of the Revd John March; the provision of accommodation for a doctors' practice in a former church hall belonging to St Peter's Church. The development of

Learning together in Handsworth. The Holyhead Association for Community Help will operate from St James' when the rebuilding is complete.

the new Handsworth group ministry will enable St James, with others, to build up its work alongside the doctors' practice in the unused part of the church hall. This latter will be based on family and child support, general advice and befriending and the development of appropriate community groups and meetings.

'Many of our church members are already very active in community life and in the caring professions and they should be supported' says the Vicar Rob Morris . . . 'which means that we should not set up complicated, wholly church-run projects, and thus add to the burden carried by already heavily committed people. We must therefore work in collaboration with others. The church's task is to identify the Kingdom not to be its identification.'

'We are near the end of the beginning!' says Rob Morris. Fifteen months of building has now been completed by local sub-contractors deliberately chosen so as to enhance local employment. 'Our life as a church has had to be a little restricted in some ways, but everything essential has continued – flourished even – despite meeting for worship, planning social events in the midst of dust, scaffolding and builder's supplies. We have learned on the way even more of the flexibility of grace.'

Soon the building will be ready for full daily use – for meetings, prayer, child care, training, family support, advice, day care for elderly and disabled people. Above all it will provide common ground, easy of access and open all day for the lively, hard pressed community of Handsworth in its rich variety of culture, language, faith and need.

The link, through the Church Urban Fund, with the extra support of R.A.F. Church of England Chaplaincies has done much more than provide the deeply appreciated provision of just under a third of the total cost. Genuine links have been forged through visits, letters – and videos! Nineteen children from the parish are spending a week at R.A.F. Gutersloh in Germany – a holiday beyond their families' hopes or means, and others are going to R.A.F. St Mawgan in Cornwall – all thanks to the generosity of R.A.F. Chaplaincy members.

The Church Urban Fund has made an award of £21,000 over three years towards further staff assistance in the parish – a Church Army Evangelist and a volunteer lay worker.

Balsall Heath Church Centre, Birmingham

Balsall Heath Church Centre is a large multi-purpose building in inner-city Birmingham. It is the home of two churches, St Paul's Church of England, and Balsall Heath United Reformed Church.

Together the two churches sponsor a variety of social and community work based at the Centre: day-care for the elderly with cooked meals served to up to 50 people per day; a visiting service for the elderly, caring for over 600 people in their own homes; youth work with evening activities, and all-day school holiday play schemes. The two churches use the premises extensively for their own activities, and many community groups also use the building.

A staff of about 20 people maintain the work of the Centre, some paid directly by the Centre, some paid by other organisations, some volunteers. Funding comes from a multiplicity of sources.

The Centre was dedicated on 12 October 1980. It was an innovative and imaginative scheme, a bold attempt to plant the Church in strength in the kind of area where it is often weak, to give the local church an adventurous mission of community service where it is often concerned mainly with self-preservation. Since 1980 the Church Centre has kept faith with its original vision, maintaining and expanding its original community services. New activities have also been added in response to local need and the Church's desire to serve. Volunteer church members now staff a coffee shop five days a week, and run a mother and toddlers club one day a week. New community groups keep coming to use the Centre's facilities: recent additions include Balsall Heath Residents Action Group, the local Police Liaison Committee and the Diocesan nationality adviser.

The Church Centre has also developed a role as a 'window on the Inner City' for the wider church. It is increasingly used for local and national conferences. Most of the Theological courses in Birmingham use the Church Centre as a base for part of their training at some time, and 3–4 theological students come for placements each year.

The co-ordination and administration of such a Centre is a demanding task. It provides a full-time job for at least one Senior member, but funding problems have meant that this role has been fulfilled in a rather 'ad hoc' way. At the outset of the project the U.R.C. Council for World Mission provided funding for a Church Centre Administrator. Then an Anglican Non-Stipendiary Minister was persuaded to come and work full time without remuneration to 'oil the wheels of the machine'.

This work is necessary for the smooth running of the project and for its effective growth to meet changing needs in the community. Local authority and voluntary bodies do not recognise such a post as something they would fund. They expect the Church to cover such work, yet this as a key role, needing a full time worker who is also a committed member of the church. Such a person has been found and has been in post since January 1986.

The total cost of the post runs currently at £11,000–12,000 per annum. The Church Centre squeezed its existing finances to provide money for this administrative post and has been aided by a two year grant of £5,000 p.a. from a U.R.C. Trust specifically to fund the Administrator/Warden. This U.R.C. funding ceased in 1988. All efforts to find other sources of funding resulted only in one donation of £250.

The Church Urban Fund has provided £30,000 over three years so that the part of Administrator/Warden can be continued.

St Peter and St Silas Lozells, Birmingham

This parish was at the heart of the Handsworth disturbances of September 1985. The population of the parish totalling some 8,300 comprises 60 per cent of Asian background, 20 per cent Afro-Caribbean and 20 per cent White.

Despite rioting all around the church, this was one building that was not touched. The area in which the church is situated is now being rebuilt and there are positive signs of an improvement in the area. Church activities are also increasing and it was for this reason that the P.C.C. started the project of an Asian Outreach Worker. The post is filled by Oliver Samuel who works in the parish with the Revd Eric Russell.

Oliver is a Christian layworker from Pakistan. He speaks Urdu and Punjabi, and this has proved invaluable in building up contacts with Muslim shopkeepers and their families, and others in the area. Oliver knows well that the job of developing relationships will be a long one. The building up of friendship and mutual trust and respect is no easy task, but it is an essential one! Though Oliver's job is a relatively new one, the ideas of it is not. A Christian bookshop was established on the Lozells Road some 11 years ago by Desmond Danzey, a former missionary of some vision. Through this shop, contacts between the local community and the local church were established, and though it was later sold to Scripture Union, the bookshop is still the base for some of Oliver's work.

The post of Asian Outreach Worker is funded for three years by a grant of £15,000 from the Church Urban Fund and by other agencies.

Oliver is establishing contacts with Asian people living within the parish, and building up friendly, sensitive and caring relationships with them. Secondly, he is instrumental in encouraging and training church members to reach out to their Asian neighbours in friendship. Finally, Oliver assists the local church in providing Christian nurture for Asian Christians who join the congregation. This can include translation facilities and advice on integration into the life of the Church, and is obviously a task requiring much insight and sensitivity.

Oliver's role as interpreter is used in many situations, and it is often more than just translating words. The customs and conventions of different cultures can need 'interpreting' too, so that understanding and mutual respect can thus develop. He has, for example, been used as interpreter by the New Testament Church of God during a mission. His skills are used at the appropriately named 'Rainbow' multi-racial playgroup at St Paul and St Silas Church, and also at the Summer Holiday Club which accommodates some 50–60 children each day for a fortnight. Oliver is used by local community agencies too for translation/communication purposes.

The job that Oliver Samuel is doing as Asian Outreach Worker, though still in its early days yet,* is meant to present the local community with a view of the Church as wanting to be involved with that community, taking cultural and religious issues seriously and with respect.

St Marks Visitors, Forest Gate, London

The parish of St Marks Forest Gate, is set within the London Borough of Newham, itself the second most deprived Local Authority in the country according to the government's own criteria. The parish has been officially designated an Urban Priority Area by the Diocese of Chelmsford and is classified as 'extremely deprived', ranking sixth from bottom in the diocesan list. The project covers not only the parish of St Marks but also the northern part of the neighbouring parish of Emmanuel Forest Gate (of which the vicar of St Marks is also Priest in Charge) which ranks as

Off to school in Newham, East London.

the most deprived parish in the whole diocese. St Marks Visitors is a neighbourhood care project totally run by local people and is designed to use the resources from within the local community in self-help. Faces are set firmly against developing this work in any way that would foster dependence on people and expertise from outside. The one factor that can make this happen is cash . . . and that is the one thing which has been provided in a small way from within, but where local resources simply cannot meet the clearly identified need. The scheme involves about thirty volunteers at any one time and consists of men and women, young and old black, white and an Asian.

The volunteers are from a variety of church backgrounds and none. St Marks operates very much as the parish church to which all sorts of denominational backgrounds are drawn to worship, the church itself is an example of a 'Christian' rather than a 'denominational' centre vying with other denominations. This is a very important factor in the whole venture. Both the church and the Visitors are a real part of the local community and are seen as the Christian workers for the area.

In 1981 a volunteer from within the church took on the role of co-ordinating volunteers who would respond to local needs, given the limitations of the time and abilities of the volunteers themselves. With publicity in English, Urdu, Gujurati, Hindi and Punjabi, the work grew rapidly. In the following year a co-ordinator was appointed full time to cope with the work load. At the time her salary was covered by a short-term grant from the D.H.S.S. Opportunities for Volunteers scheme. Since then a number of 'one off' grants have kept the project going from a variety of sources, but each of these has dried up and at present the only source of income is £1,500 for the next two years, the rest being underwritten by the church council as an act of faith.

In 1986 over 1,600 referrals were dealt with by the Visitors. Requests come from social workers, doctors, home helps, neighbours, family, local councillors, health visitors. The cases have included arranging temporary foster care, helping illegal immigrants to normalise their position, arranging Christmas parties for the housebound, finding accommodation, baby sitting, shopping, visiting the bereaved, sick, elderly, hospital visits, small removals, light domestic repairs, gardening, literacy tuition, translation work, helping battle through bureaucracy, legal advice. Sometimes the volunteer can deal with the matter personally, sometimes another local person is contacted and sometimes an outside agency is brought in to help. From the sheer quantity of requests for help and the nature of the cases, it will be seen that the project is a major contributor to the self-reliance and practical mutual help developing within the local community.

About thirty volunteers are trained and encouraged by being carefully selected for particular visits, and then by reflecting on what has happened. There are no preparation courses, as those often simply 'deskill' local people out of their innate understanding of issues. The proof of the success of the scheme lies in:

the vast and increasing number of cases,
the increasing use by other voluntary and statutory bodies,
the success rate of dealing with the vast majority of cases,
the fact that every single case is dealt with from within the local community . . . this is vitally important.

In 1987 the Vicar and P.C.C. of St Marks, who act as the sponsoring and managing body, reviewed progress and decided that, from September 1987, the work can best be developed by:

The routine secretarial work being done by a volunteer member.

The full-time employee being freed from the secretarial work to concentrate more on the more sensitive cases, of which the number is considerable, and to develop, for example, the pensioners lunch club.

The appointment of an Asian community worker. At present there is just one Asian member among the volunteers who speaks only Urdu. It is vital for the Visitors to move from being a mainly black and white group to be seen to be able to relate freely and offer help to the Asian community.

The Visitors obviously work very closely with the church as a whole. At present there are 25 different activities each week in the church centre, ranging from playgrounds to pensioners clubs. In an area where less than half the households own a car and where pedestrians simply will not venture out at night, the addition of a minibus would greatly enhance the work of all that is done.

The Church Urban Fund has made a grant towards the development of the work of St Marks Visitors of £45,300 over three years.

10

Church Growth and Renewal

There is no such thing as the 'classic' story of church growth or renewal. There is no method of working which will have the same success everywhere. Many clergy will know that ideas which have worked well and have brought success in one parish will not take off when tried in their next parish. Many lay people in parishes are now learning how to grow without a full-time clergyman of their own.

Social and economic conditions vary from place to place. People in churches and communities differ so widely, and will have such different histories that what they hope for, and what will bring a response, will be quite different. There are shelves of books about church goods which describe how growth and renewal can be or has been brought about. *Faith in the City* was both realistic and visionary in what it hoped for and in what should be the characteristics of a parish within a U.P.A. The Christian community of the parish should be local, outward looking, participative and ecumenical. It also began with realism by recommending a parish audit. Only when the history and characteristics of a parish are revealed and understood can plans for growth and renewal be made, based on fact rather than fantasy.

St Barnabas, Blackburn

One church community which has demonstrated realism, hard work and vision in its own idiosyncratic way is St Barnabas in Blackburn – 'The church in the Co-Op'. After the original Victorian church was demolished, the congregation moved into the local school and then purchased an empty Co-operative supermarket. This was subsequently converted into a church and community centre, hence the name.

The parish of St Barnabas is one of Victorian terraces with its streets sloping down towards the city centre. The small congregation worshipped in a room built onto the side of the school. It seemed to the Diocese like a possible candidate for amalgamation with the surrounding parishes. In one of those enlightened strokes of foolish Anglican genius, the Diocese appointed the Revd Herrick Daniel as Priest in Charge to 'see what he could do'. He is a priest of West Indian origin with an energy-filled, charismatic personality. Under his guidance and 'prayerful bullying' the congregation began to grow and to make new plans. Herrick Daniel takes up what happened next in his own words:

'The story began when a friend of mine by the name of Mr Bryan Winden from Gib Lane, Livesey, Blackburn, who was then a member of St Barnabas Church, came to see me in the vicarage at 24 Adelaide Terrace, towards the end of a bright week about four and a half years ago. Towards the end of a casual evening, he said to me "Herrick, it would be nice if there was an old factory within the parish of St Barnabas boundary that I could convert into a church!" I signalled my approval by replying that it would be a very good idea. We talked about it for about two or more minutes and concluded by Bryan saying to me to keep my eyes open for such a building. A day or more later, Bryan rang me at the vicarage to inform me that, following our conversation about the idea of a factory for a church, he has, incidentically, seen in the *Evening Telegraph* that the Co-Op at 85 Johnston Street was on the market for sale, so could I follow this up. I immediately made some initial enquiries about it from the Floor Manager, who confirmed that the building was for sale and the Management was willing to accept a reasonable offer.

'I eventually found out through the Co-Op agent that they wanted £70,000 for the building, by then the Church did not have a single pound to put down on the building, as St Barnabas Church had, a matter of days previously, completed the debts of the small church extension built on to the day school, costing in the region of £16,000.

'I brought the idea of purchasing the Co-Op building to the Church Council and the general congregation, but the idea was dismissed because they said that we did not have the money.

'I then approached the Diocese of Blackburn to ask for help. At first the Diocese could not see how it would be possible for a supermarket to be changed into a church and community centre, but I was so persistent to show how such a project would help the church people and the community as a whole that they decided to follow this up and to see if they could help. By the time they had finished a series of committee meetings, the building was sold to someone else. The whole idea was then forgotten and pushed aside.

'About six months later, I received a telephone call from the new owner of the Co-Op who explained that he understood that I was interested in the building. He said that the purpose for which he bought the building had now been changed, and he would like to sell it to me. I asked for the price, he said £90,000. I complained that he bought it for £70,000 and that after only six months to ask £90,000 was a bit too much. He agreed to reduce the price to £82,000.

'The idea raised new interest and excitement in me. I went back to the church to explain how we could change this two floor building into a church and community centre. Again, the church people thought that we could not afford it. It took me about six months to teach, preach and convince the people in the church through Bible Study, literature and arguments that if we depend upon God totally through faith in Him, I believed that God would supply all the money we needed. Towards the end of the six months, most people did believe me and started praying with me for the cause. Meanwhile, I was putting pressure on the Diocese of Blackburn through every channel I knew that would influence them to help us out financially. Eventually, they decided to buy the building for us on condition that we would convert it ourselves, to which I said yes. It cost £82,000 to purchase, plus £2,500 legal fees.'

There was then the enormous task of raising the money to adapt the building. The congregation took up the challenge with energy. As well as considerable local fund-raising, their great claim to fame is the photo auction. They wrote to every celebrity imaginable, Henry Kissinger, Elizabeth Taylor, Margaret Thatcher, the cast of Coronation Street and many more for signed photographs. The auction of these gave St Barnabas and its cause a great deal of publicity. A local workman took on the task of supervision of the renovation once plans had been drawn up and agreed with an architect.

The church and centre is now up and running and it is a hive of activity all day and for seven days a week. It is a tribute to what can be done in an area with all the characteristics of a U.P.A. Unemployment is at 9.7 per cent, very many houses are overcrowded, there is a high percentage of one-parent families and elderly people. There are many homes lacking basic amenities. There is a particularly high percentage of households where the head of the house was born in the New Commonwealth or Pakistan.

St Barnabas tries to meet the needs of these residents. Particularly, the Co-Op Church has a lounge and kitchen area which provides warmth, company and food for a range of different groups of people throughout the day. Behind this area there is a playgroup with a retired Asian lady doctor as a helper. There is also a Christian book and record shop which brings outsiders to the church. The hall downstairs is increasingly used by local groups, especially the disabled.

Most of the money for St Barnabas was raised before the Fund came on the scene, but in 1989 £15,000 over three years was awarded towards running expenses.

St Oswald's Church, Bidston, Birkenhead

This Merseyside parish is dominated by the Ford and Ballantyre estates. Here unemployment is around 48 per cent for the male population, the crime rate is high, and there is considerable drug abuse.

St Oswald's Church stands in a prominent position, and can be seen from both council estates and much of the rest of the parish. Church members can see that it provides a natural focus for the community, and want to make their church more suitable to serve that community, with all its needs. They decided to divide off the rear part of the church and create rooms for community activity. The vicar, the Revd Paul Kirby, describes how they raised the funds for the work:

'We launched our appeal on All Saint's Day, Sunday 1 November 1987, with a Congregational "Gift Day". We did not feel able to ask others for help until we had shown our own willingness to "put our money where our mouth is" as a Church Family. This gift day brought in the staggering sum (at least for our people, many of whom are poor and unemployed) of over £10,000 given or promised.

'Then, as word of our appeal spread, money began to come in from many friends and link churches. £30,000 became available for the project when the Charity Commission gave us permission to use the fire insurance money which had been invested since the time, over ten years ago, when our parish hall was burnt down by vandals. Many trusts have responded most generously, and our main "link parish" of Heswall promised us £8,000. We had over £82,000 either promised or given for the work – enough to complete the building side of our scheme.'

Since the completion of alterations, St Oswald's Church Centre has become a focal point for many people all around the area. Some come for specific meetings or groups, others just for a chat over tea and coffee. One way or another St Oswald's is now open – seven days a week!

The Church Urban Fund contributes £54,900 for the salary of a community worker. The grant is spread over three years.

The church's prominent position set on a hill between housing estates means that it acts like a beacon in the area. It is certainly a focal point for a growing number of community activities.

There is a Mother and Baby Clinic on Friday afternoons, staffed by a doctor, nurses and health visitors. Welfare foods are also on sale with tea and coffee provided. A mums and toddler's group has been formed and demand means another one may begin soon. Many people come along for help or advice over a variety of different matters. The Centre is manned by a team of volunteers who serve tea and coffee throughout the day.

Paul Kirby and his curate, Charles Royden, a former police constable, spend a large amount of their time in the Centre. The attractive parish leaflet describes their work:

WELFARE RIGHTS

Once Charlie Morris was disabled and felt useless. Now that misery has changed and he feels great peace and happiness as a result of his faith in God. Now that he is well he had dedicated his life to helping people, using his ability as a welfare rights worker.

There are many problems which are easily solved when you speak with someone like Charlie Morris who is used to dealing with them. Social Security benefits, housing problems, representation at tribunals, entitlements to help, these are just some of the problems which he understands. Charlie has developed excellent relations with the Social Services and knows the quickest way to sort out most difficulties which can occur. Often people are unaware of what help may be available to them and he can suggest help ranging from free bedding for incontinence sufferers to meals for the elderly.

A problem shared is a problem halved so call in and speak to Charlie Morris about anything in complete and absolute confidence. There is no charge for his help and all you have to do is ask.

Charlie Morris is available at St Oswald's Tuesday and Thursday.

St Oswald's Community Newsheet boasts of its activities:

CREDIT UNION

History was made on Wednesday 25th January when residents in the parish came together in the church centre to become the first members of the Ford and Ballantyne Credit Union. Months of hard work under the guidance of Kathleen Stansfield, Wirral's community Credit Union development worker are now paying off. Not only are church members helping to run the Credit Union but the church itself will be used as a place to pay money in, and to join. We have been working closely with Father O'Riordan of St Paul's Roman Catholic Church and the Credit Union will be another sign of our mutual friendship and support. As the community Associations and all other groups in the parish join together the Credit Union will be an excellent way to unite the community in this worthwhile cause.

Now there will be no need to pay extra in shops for H.P. Neither will you have to pay a fortune to loan money and be told where you can spend it. Soon we hope to make these kinds of shops and loan companies in Birkenhead a thing of the past. By joining your Credit Union you can help put them out of business.

One man who took a loan for £80 from a Birkenhead loan company found he had to pay back £250 in weekly payments which he couldn't afford. He came to St Oswald's for advice and managed to get the problem sorted out. When he realised how much he had been charged for the loan he said: 'I feel like I have been mugged'. Of course that is what credit, or debt can be like – except this form of robbery is legal.

By joining the Credit Union you can save and borrow and it won't cost hardly anything. The Union is run voluntarily, by the members for the members. Nobody makes any money – so it's cheap. By joining the Credit Union you will be fighting the debt trap as well as strengthening the local community. So call at St Oswald's Church Centre now and ask to join. And remember if you are in money trouble don't panic – call at the Church Centre and ask to speak to one of the staff team for confidential advice. *They can help.*

EDUCATION

One person you may meet at St Oswalds is Graham Rogers who works for Wirral Metropolitan College. He is organising activities out of the main college sites and into the community itself. Typing, cookery, Health and Beauty are just some of the classes that he has started following suggestions from people in the parish. Most classes are held when children are in school and there is a creche provided for younger children. There will be opportunities to work towards skills with recognised qualifications. Anyone wishing to join a course or to have a new course started should see Graham. Remember you don't have to be a 'Brain of Britain' the classes are fun – not a school. So get in touch soon – you don't know what you're missing.

Paul Kirby began his life as a Conservative Evangelical. He still holds to that tradition. But, faced with the enormous social problems of a parish like this, he has opened the doors to all comers. There is no doubting the Christian ethos of the centre. Its first aim is to help those in need. This is a gospel which speaks through actions rather than words.

Benchill Ecumenical Service Scheme (B.E.S.S.), Wythenshawe, Manchester

Many churches are not ambitious enough in their planning for the future. This cannot be said of the Benchill Scheme on the vast Wythenshawe estate outside Manchester.

Four out of ten 19 year olds referred to Wythenshawe Hospital are into their third pregnancy. Most of them come from the Benchill area of Wythenshawe in south Manchester. All of Wythenshawe is an urban priority area, but Benchill contains the most concentrated level of deprivation.

There is an undercurrent of violence in Benchill, which is part of the largest housing estate in Western Europe built on a scale that defeats community life. Elderly people go in fear of mugging and crime is generated by the high level of unemployment and the large

A room with a view – the Benchill Estate, Wythenshawe.

and growing drug problem. Shared needles have already produced the first AIDS victims.

The severe emotional difficulties suffered by local people mean that they cannot provide leadership skills; people have no energy to use to improve their own lives. The Revd Oliver Forshaw, vicar of St Luke's Church, Benchill, estimates that at least 90 per cent of present communicants need or have needed 'sustained pastoral care before being able to exercise any effective ministry towards others'.

To take action on these interwoven problems, three local churches – Anglican, Methodist and Roman Catholic – are jointly sponsoring an ambitious three-year ecumenical pilot scheme to strengthen the existing missionary outreach of the congregations. They have employed skilled lay leaders to encourage local talent and initiative in the hope that they will be able to prepare for the time when they will be no longer needed. The Benchill Ecumenical Service Scheme is now commonly known by all involved at B.E.S.S.

The Church Urban Fund has agreed to pay £80,000 over three years towards B.E.S.S., and the local Methodist and Catholic churches are seeking ways of providing additional finance. All three churches are making available premises to house the project and its workers.

They share similar experiences. Each church has falling congregations with faithful elderly members not being replaced by younger people. The ministers agree that depression and apathy is widespread among local people.

Oliver Forshaw says: 'The whole church has to face the question of local leadership. You have loads of talent in the middle class suburban areas, whether in church or the wider community, that variety of talent is lacking in our area where it is most needed. It seems we cannot persuade either clergy or lay people to bring their talents into these areas.'

Father George Browne, priest of St John and St Thomas Catholic Church says the 'communal despair' of Benchill is probably no greater than anywhere else; just less disguised. But that does mean that the project will require people of special talents, willing to work flexibly.

The Revd Wesley Fairhurst, minister of Brownley Green Methodist Church, says his church is 'so down on its rear end' that the congregation has accepted the idea of the scheme 'on the condition that it is not going to involve them in any more work'.

There is a great deal of existing work in the three congregations to build on. The Catholics run a summer play scheme, knowing that it will keep their school free of vandalism for a few weeks. St Luke's has been running a community programme since 1978, financed by central and local government, which includes personal counselling and providing space for a variety of groups at the church hall.

Each Wednesday, pensioners come in after morning service for a chat over a cup of coffee and biscuits, and mothers and toddlers use the hall later in the day as a relief from their daily lives. But the mums stay away if the topic of the day is AIDS, or if they know that strangers will be there. Only incapacity would keep the pensioners away.

Mary Harrop, a lively 75 year old, is the centre of one group, keeping them creased with laughter. She exchanges favourite paperbacks with her friends, handing them over in paper bags as if they were on some kind of censored list. Like most of the pensioners, Mary comes for the company which she continues outside the coffee mornings with bus trips to nearby markets with the friends she makes there.

Oliver says: 'It is fair to say we have won the confidence of the folk we already work with' but adds that it is extremely slow and difficult. *Faith in the City* provided the spur for the three churches to sponsor a joint initiative which will include counselling work of the kind that Oliver and his wife, Jean, a trained counsellor, have found has borne fruit with the lives of individual people.

Young parents, they have found, can be helped despite the enormous odds. Oliver says it is at the point where young adults see their children started into school and become conscious of how much violence there is around 'that they begin to wake up to the fact that the church is important and can do something for them'.

'We are conscious that the Gospel can make sense to them at that stage, and we need to be doing something to help them as parents so that human life is strengthened and they are not just tiny households in a sea of indifference in a very unjust, callous society. The job is a community building task.'

The hope is 'that we shall equip enough local talent to ensure that the congregational life will go forward into the 90s in a much more competent way than has been the case for twenty years'.

The ecumenical aspect of the scheme is important for the well being of the entire church, says Oliver. 'Christians know deep within themselves that the denominational divisions are offensive to God and they are weakening the impact of the Gospel,' he says. 'If we are going to convince the public that the Church has got something vital then we have got to show that these terrible divisions can be broken through.'

Oliver hopes it can become a self-supporting scheme, but points out that the monochrome nature of Benchill places it at a greater disadvantage than many areas. But he has no doubts about why the Church is involved.

'The Church need to be doing this,' he says. 'Because we are on the spot, we are more of a community than any other group despite all our weakness and inadequacies. We have a motivation based on the Gospel which no other agency has, so we are prepared to stick at it in the face of all the difficulties. And there is a spiritual resource that only the church can harness.'

The four community workers at the B.E.S.S. project are Margaret Parker, Jo Johnson, Sue O'Brien and Fiona Timothy. Already things are happening.

The combined, newly-discovered musical talent of the local churches took to the streets in a Good Friday Open Air Witness; young people's groups are meeting and Sue has been invited to set up a youth counselling service in one of the secondary schools.

Life around the derelict and vandalised Haveley Circle shopping area in Benchill, Wythenshawe near Manchester.

Mums struggling on their own with young children now meet together at new self-help 'Parents Alone Group' – supported by local health visitors and the probation service. B.E.S.S. is involved in playgroups and mother and toddlers groups. Contacts can be made, problems followed up, and the introduction of music and movement has created new excitement and enthusiasm – amongst parents and children. Keep fit groups at local church centres have really taken off. So much so, that when Fiona, the Keep Fit leader, was on holiday, one of the local mums felt confident enough to take over!

Those who find the impressive Wythenshawe Civic Centre rather overwhelming are discovering new activities and making new friends at their local church.

After the success of a drama workshop, there are now regular sessions at one of the churches. As well as giving new vitality to worship, people are discovering that they have something to contribute, and can express emotions which have been hidden for years. One of the most important parts of the work is to train, support and encourage local people and local Christians to continue and extend the scheme in the future.

Together, the churches of Benchill are discovering what it means to be the presence of Christ in the community.

Mary was a prisoner in her own home. She was depressed and suffered from panic attacks. Although she desperately wanted to return to the mother and toddler group she once attended, she was too afraid to get outside the front door.

She was visited by a counsellor from B.E.S.S. who offered understanding, support and encouragement – and also a lift to the mother and toddler group when Mary wanted it.

One day, Mary and baby Thomas greeted her at the door, ready to go out! For the next three months, they were given a lift to the group. With the support of her counsellor in an office nearby, she has gradually gained in confidence and self-respect.

She's come a long way. She and Thomas now travel alone on the bus, reassured by the knowledge that her counsellor will be there when she arrives. There's a lot of patient work required before Mary becomes fully independent, but she's making good progress.

Through B.E.S.S. she has gained self-esteem and confidence because someone has loved and accepted her, encouraged her, respected her fragility and stuck with her.

Dorothy lives alone, in a high rise block. Radio, television and her two cats were the only companions in a lonely, isolated world. Stories in her local newspaper warned her about the crime that haunted the streets and alleys of her once friendly neighbourhood. Locks and bolts were unable to keep out the fear which was

Keeping fit and happy – with BESS.

invading her home. The little security and comfort she had left was gradually being destroyed.

After regular visits from a member of the pastoral visiting team, Dorothy has begun to get out. She has made new friends at the keep fit club.

'In the war we couldn't get out at night because the bombs were dropping, now we can't get out for fear of getting mugged!', she joked with Margaret. 'At least we can come here and have a good moan!'

She's also joined the newly formed craft club and is even talking about going out to one of the united evening services with some of her new found friends!

B.E.S.S. is bringing hope to people like Dorothy – helping them find new life, light and hope in their community.

The Manor Ecumenical Parish, Sheffield

The Parish of Sheffield Manor is an Urban Priority Area in Sheffield which is made up of local authority housing estates largely dating from the 1920s and 1930s. Many of them are decayed and some are being rebuilt. It is a classic 'outer housing estate' with its centre some two miles from the city. There is a serious problem of unemployment following the collapse of the city steel industry in the early 1980s. The parish also has a high incidence of unskilled workers, single, elderly and single-parent families.

The Manor Parish is a Local Ecumenical Project with ten congregations – five Anglican, four Methodists and one Baptist. Seven of these congregations have less than 25 members, including all the four on the Manor Estate itself. Two of these, (Anglican and Methodist), worship in a single small building (Methodist owned) on the lower part of the estate. Until 1977 St Swithun's Church acted as a centre for Upper Manor, and to an extent for the whole estate. The church was then declared unsafe and pulled down. After various difficulties the congregation of some 15 now worship in a room in the vicarage. In 1985 the neighbouring Baptist Church had to be demolished, and its congregation – also some 15 – worship in a hired room. The two congregations also share worship frequently.

On the Manor shops lie derelict, houses open to the sky, playgrounds vandalised and open spaces full of rubbish. Within this context there is determination, humour and life. What is needed are signs of hope, and the Church can help to fulfil this, demonstrating that Christians care about the people of Manor, believe that they are worth serving, and are prepared to invest in their future. Local Christians have worked, prayed and lived on Manor over the years, supported by a series of Team Vicars at St Swithun's. Richard Atkinson, the present Team Vicar, arrived in July 1987. They are convinced that this is a point at which there is a need for the wider church to provide help for this determined but beleaguered group of Christians.

The project seeks to provide a church building to serve the needs of the Manor Estate. It will be a Church of England owned building, with an agreement under the Sharing of Church Buildings Act with the Baptist Church. There will be opportunity for the city Social Services Department to use a room as an interviewing centre, and for groups such as tenants' associations, play groups and lunch clubs to use the hall area in an area tragically deprived of resources. The project has enthusiastic backing from tenants' groups and co-operation with Family and Community Services is a part of the work in the area. The City Council funded employment agency, M.A.T.R.E.C. (Manor Training and Resources Centre), has also given support. The lack of resources in the area means that a fundamental part of the work is the supply of places to meet, worship with local groups of different backgrounds and emphases. The project is rooted in the local community and is the determined brain-child of local Christians.

This estate is being systematically 'gutted' and rebuilt. The Church has an opportunity to play its part in the renewal of the Manor community, and to continue the heroic work which Christians have been doing there since the 1940s. Those who know Sheffield also know that for the churches 'The Manor' has always been a place of hope and experiment.

There is good local funding for the rebuilding of St Swithun's and the Church Urban Fund has made a capital contribution of £50,000.

The final paragraph of Sheffield's submission to the Fund is very important. If the name were changed, what they say of The Manor could be said of almost every other place described in this book. For outsiders reading about life in U.P.A. parishes, it is possibly the most important paragraph in the whole book.

'It was felt that there was a stigma and bad reputation attached to living on the estate. When Manor's problems were discussed with people from outside the area, the reaction was often "well, what do you expect if you live on The Manor?" Some fieldworkers said that tenants had told them they had often experienced this attitude in dealing with public service agency staff. The attitude was that Manor is a place where problem families live, therefore if you live on the estate you are regarded as a problem. It was said that this attitude can only be overcome by staff training and publicity to demonstrate how a family can have problems forced upon it. That is to say, it should be seen as a family with problems as opposed to assuming all Manor's families are "problem families".'

11

Taking Stock

By the end of 1989 the Fund had raised over £12 million. It has spent £5.2 million on over 200 projects. What difference has it made? Can examples of change and improvement be given? Those who have raised the money would like to know not only where it has gone but also something of the effect the Fund has had on poverty and hardship in England. Previous chapters which detail some of the projects are a testimony in themselves to the worth of the venture. They support work which is already going on which will help to change the face of our country.

The work of the Church Urban Fund is also set in a wider context, that of a changing Britain in a dramatically changing Europe. The Archbishop has continued to hold a central place in the debates about change. In doing so he has continued to attract the criticism of a conservative press, and conservative journalists, as he has tried to steer and guide the Anglican Church through a programme of revision and change.

As a person and as a national figure he has held his ground on the issues raised by *Faith in the City*. In October 1989 he was interviewed by Carol Kennedy, Deputy Editor of *The Director*. She wrote of him:

> 'He sees a risk of the successful becoming like the Pharisees, self-righteous and "judgemental" in their attitudes to the unsuccessful. The "obsession" of many young people with making money quickly makes him uneasy, along with the fear that a generation of hard-edged achievers may prove less sympathetic than present business leaders to what he calls "the left-behinds, the casualties of success".
>
> "I resist the idea," says Runcie with feeling, "that the only driving dynamic of society is self-interest." At a later stage in the conversation he speaks of the strain on community structures when "we put our competitive demands before the needs of others".'

The Archbishop visiting the Karate club at the Emmanuel Church, Bolton, in February 1989.

A direct response

Most interesting to observe is that in spite of the controversial recommendations of *Faith in the City* and the remarks critical of social and political trends made by the Archbishop, the Church Urban Fund is achieving its targets. Why is this? Could it be that the churchgoing public can see beyond the partisan conclusions of the Commissioners and the energy absorbing debates of the Church and recognise the real cries of human need coming from urban areas? That has been my experience of promoting the Fund in a market town and in a rural Diocese.

Political prejudices have not been apparent in the fund-raising work. Rural and urban communities have responded equally well to the targets they have been given. Many have used the campaign also as an educational exercise. U.P.A. parishes have had too many requests for visits and for 'links'. In a way hardly ever seen before, Anglicans of all shades have given to one particular charity. Fund raising events have been most imaginative and very successful. The stories are many of individuals, in town or village, with or without the support of their incumbent, saying, 'we must do something about this', and getting on with it. Church Urban Fund Week gave an extra opportunity for initiative, though Bishops and Archdeacons say they are still tripping over boxes of candles in the less tidy vestries!

Ecumenical projects

One of the criticisms of *Faith in the City* is that it was an Anglican report. There is nothing denominational about the projects which are supported by the Fund. The only necessary Anglican thing about them is that they have to be commended by the Diocesan Bishop. Projects described here, and very many more now being supported by the Fund, arise from the initiatives of several churches working together. Others are from local non-church groups which have Church backing and involvement. It is very clear that when Christians are responding to a local need, denominational barriers are soon forgotten. It is only when we stay with internal church affairs that we seem determined to continue with a series of self-inflicted wounds.

As newly constituted county and national bodies emerge from a restructured British Council of Churches it will continue to be in local co-operation that the strength of inter-church work will be based. Within the limited number of examples in this book Baptist, Methodist and Roman Catholic projects have received support from the Fund. Ecumenism will only be real and long-lasting if the local church has taken co-operation into its system. People begin this process not necessarily with doctrinal debates, important as they are, but with getting to know one another and by working together. The Church Urban Fund has been able to support and encourage this co-operation.

Churchmanship diminished

In a Church of England divided by internal party strife it is striking that this is absent from descriptions of projects in this book. Party allegiances are hardly ever mentioned and where they are, it is only to demonstrate that overriding social need has forced the individuals concerned on to a wider understanding of their faith.

Faith in the City and the Church Urban Fund may well be understood as God's vehicles to allow the gospel to break through in the guise of those in need just when the clutches of party rivalry threaten to do their worst. Because projects come from so many different kinds of churches they give a new context in which theology can emerge. If theology literally means 'God's word to us' then it has been heard throughout this whole enterprise. Those who have the ability must now stand back and interpret the consequences of this word for the rest of us.

A new theology?

It is just not true that there was a weakness in the theology which was embodied in *Faith in the City*. The emphasis of its chapters and the confidence with which recommendations were made demonstrate clearly what the authors thought was the place of the Christian religion and of a national church in English society in the late twentieth century. The lack of actual theological propositions and of a position 'domesticated' by the members of the Commission has allowed many other groups to continue working at the theological issues which arise from the report.

Anthony Harvey, the theologian on the Commission, has since edited a collection of essays from people who have a variety of religious backgrounds called *Theology in the City* (published by S.P.C.K., 1989. ISBN 0-281-04417-1). Books like this raise the question of whether there should be a special theology of or for the inner-city or whether it is better that all our theology should be renewed by these insights.

An underclass revealed?

Since the publication of *Faith in the City* a new phrase has come into use – social underclass. It is an ugly and offensive term which smacks of class prejudice and paternalism. Yet it is a way of describing many who live in U.P.A.s. It is not used for the poor who are 'going through a bad time' because of illness, unemployment or because they happen to live in homes which are poorly built.

Underclass is used not just to describe people who are poor, it describes a kind of poverty. It is more about a type of behaviour than overwhelming material circumstances. Writing in *The Sunday Times* in November 1989 the political scientist Charles Murray produced a feature defining the underclass in this way. He chose the example of his experience in his home town in the United States to illustrate what he was saying:

'Then there was another set of people, just a handful of them. These poor didn't lack just money. They were defined by their behaviour. Their homes were littered and unkempt. The men in the family were unable to hold a job for more than a few weeks at a time. Drunkenness was common. The children grew up ill-schooled and ill-behaved and contributed a disproportionate share of the local juvenile delinquents.'

Such people and families are no strangers to the churches and to Christian workers who have been trying to help when no-one else could since the middle of the last century. Every vicarage doorstep in England has been worn down a little by their feet. *Faith in the City* has brought the fate of these people to the attention of the nation. Thank God the churches never used underclass to describe them. Now that this deeper kind of poverty and deprivation has been brought into the open perhaps more systematic attempts at help and understanding will be given. The evidence is not yet there. The pressure must be kept up.

What future for the Fund?

One of the Church of England's greatest difficulties is coping with success. In other cultures and enterprises hard work and initiative are welcomed with acclaim. Within the churches such things are suspect and disturbing. The staff of the Church Urban Fund have worked with great flourish. They have produced attractive materials, they have set targets for Dioceses and they have given publicity to ambitious projects. Will this level of campaigning activity be kept up once the financial targets are met?

A major question of policy now faces the Trustees. When the fund-raising work is completed what kind of a fund should this be? The Trustees could settle for being solely a grant-making trust, responding to applications which come within their charitable terms. They could choose to publicise projects so that the pressing social issues could be kept before the public eye. More assertively, the Fund could become a home version of Oxfam or Christian Aid and take a full part in debates about the future of our nation.

By continuing to make sizeable grants the Trustees are exercising considerable political influence. The Church Urban Fund already ranks high in the league table of major national trusts. Will the Church of England keep its nerve and use the Fund as an arm of its own social lobbying, or will it be embarrassed by its own success and back off into the quieter waters of 'doing good'?

The story so far has been confident and assertive. What of the future? Perhaps God will not allow the Church to weaken this great piece of work. Just perhaps, *Faith in the City* and the Church Urban Fund will be seen as a turning-point in the rediscovery of God's mission for the Church.

APPENDIX I
Summary of Main Recommendations of Faith in the City

To the Church of England

1. A national system for designating U.P.A. parishes should be developed.

2. Dioceses should devote greater attention to the effective collection and presentation of accurate statistics.

3. The internal distribution of clergy by dioceses should be adjusted where necessary to ensure that U.P.A. parishes receive a fair share, and particular attention should be paid in this respect to parishes on large outer estates.

4. Dioceses should explore the possibilities of fresh stipendiary lay ministries, not necessarily tied to one parish.

5. The 'Audit for the Local Church' which we propose should be further developed, and adopted by local U.P.A. churches.

6. In urban areas the deanery should have an important support and pastoral planning function.

7. Each parish should review, preferably annually, what progress in co-operation has been made between clergy and laity, between Churches, and ecumenically, with the aim of developing partnership in ministry.

8. Appointments should be made to the Boards and Councils of the General Synod, and a new Commission on Black Anglican Concerns established, to enable the Church to make a more effective response to racial discrimination and disadvantage, and to the alienation experienced by many black people in relation to the Church of England.

9. The General Synod should consider how a more appropriate system of representation which pays due regard to minority interests can be implemented for the Synod elections of 1990.

10. The appropriate Church voluntary bodies should consider how schemes for voluntary service in U.P.A.s could be extended to widen the age range of those eligible, and to allow for part-time as well as full-time volunteering.

11. Dioceses with significant concentrations of U.P.A.s should initiate Church Leadership Development Programmes.

12. Our proposals for an extension of Local Non-Stipendiary Ministry, including those relating to selection, training and funding, should be tested in dioceses, and monitored over a ten-year period.

13. All dioceses should manifest a commitment to post-ordination training and continued ministerial education in U.P.A.s, to the extent at least of regular day-release courses.

14. Urgent attention should be given to appropriate training for teachers and supervisors in all areas of theological education, particularly those concerned with ministry in U.P.A.s, and to the provision of theological and educational resources in urban centres.

15. A.C.C.M. should be adequately funded to promote and monitor officially sanctioned experiments in theological education.

16. A.C.C.M. should be given power, in certain defined cases, to direct candidates to specific courses of training, and bishops should endorse such direction.

17. The role of non-residential training courses similar to the Aston Scheme should be further developed.

18. Dioceses and deaneries should undertake a reappraisal of their support systems for U.P.A. clergy.

19. The Liturgical Commission should pay close attention to the liturgical needs of Churches in the U.P.A.s.

20. A reassessment of the traditional patterns of the Church's work of nurture of young people in U.P.A.s is required at parish, deanery and diocesan level.

21. Sharing agreements with other denominations should be adopted more widely, as should the informal sharing of church buildings (other than the church itself) with those of other faiths.

22. In cases of the sale of redundant churches, there should be earlier and more open consultation with community organizations and bodies such as housing associations when future uses are being considered.

23. The historic resources of the Church should be redistributed between dioceses to equalize the capital and income resources behind each clergyman, deaconess and licensed lay worker in the stipendiary ministry. The redistribution formula should take account of potential giving.

24. Within dioceses, the acute financial needs of the U.P.A. churches require a clear response.

25. A Church Urban Fund should be established to strengthen the Church's presence and promote the Christian witness in the U.P.A.s.

26. The Church of England should continue to question the morality of economic policies in the light of their effects.

27. Churches should take part in initiatives to engage unemployed people in U.P.A.s in job-creating projects. The use of church premises for this purpose must be encouraged.

28. The Church should build on good practice in ministry to unemployed people: Industrial Mission has an important role to play here.

29. We recommend the use of properly-trained social workers working with local churches and neighbourhood groups as an important part of the total ministry of the Church in the U.P.A.s.

30. Church social workers should be trained within the mainstream of social work, but with particular attention paid to the character and

needs of social work in the church context. The Church should initiate discussion with social work training agencies to this end.

31. Dioceses should, through their Boards for Social Responsibility, develop and support community work, and should exercise a strategic role in support of local programmes in their U.P.A.

32. Discussions should be held between the General Synod Board for Social Responsibility and the British Council of Churches Community Work Advisory Committee with a view to strengthening the national support networks for community work. The Church of England should be prepared to devote central resources to this end.

33. Additional Church-sponsored urban studies centres for teacher training should be established.

34. All diocesan Boards and Councils of Education should give special priority to the needs of the U.P.A. schools for which they are responsible.

35. The governors and managers of Church schools should consider whether composition of foundation governors in the school adequately reflects the ethnic constituency of its catchment area.

36. Consideration should be given to a further exploration of the ecumenical dimension at secondary level, including the possibility of establishing Church of England/Roman Catholic schools in U.P.A.s, which would offer a significant proportion of places to children of other faiths.

37. A review of the Diocesan Education Committee measures should be undertaken, to allow the formulation of Diocesan policies for church schools on admission criteria and other issues, such as religious education and worship, equal opportunities and community education.

38. The General Synod's Board of Education, in consultation with Diocesan Youth Officers, should move towards a national strategy for the Church's work with young people in U.P.A.s, and initiate and support work specifically within these areas.

To Government and Nation

1, A greater priority for the outer estates is called for within urban policy initiatives.

2. The resources devoted to Rate Support Grant should be increased in real terms, and within the enhanced total a greater bias should be given to the U.P.A.s. Efficiency audits should be used to tackle wasteful expenditure.

3. The size of the Urban Programme should be increased, and aspects of its operation reviewed.

4. The concept of 'Partnership' in the U.P.A.s should be developed by central and local government to promote greater consultation with, and participation by, local people at neighbourhood level.

5. There should be a new deal between government and the voluntary sector, to provide long-term continuity and funding for recognised voluntary bodies working alongside statutory agencies.

6. A new impetus should be given to support for small firms in U.P.A.s, perhaps by the establishment of a Council for Small Firms in Urban Areas.

7. There should be additional job-creating public expenditure in the U.P.A.s on capital and current account.

8. The Government should promote more open public discussion about the current levels of overtime working.

9. The Community Programme eligibility rules and other constraints, including pay limits, should be relaxed, particularly to encourage greater participation by women and unemployed people with families to support.

10. The Community Programme should be expanded to provide 500,000 places.

11. The Government should extend to those unemployed for more than a year eligibility for the long-term rate of Supplementary Benefit, or an equivalent enhanced rate of income support under whatever new arrangements may be introduced.

12. The present level of Child Benefit should be increased as an effective means of assisting, without stigma, families in poverty.

13. The present level of 'earnings disregards' in relation to Unemployment Benefit and Supplementary Benefit should be increased to mitigate the effects of the poverty and unemployment traps.

14. The Government should establish an independent enquiry to undertake a wide-ranging review of the inter-relationship between income support, pay and the taxation system.

15. Ethnic records should be kept and monitored by public housing authorities, as a step towards eliminating direct and indirect discrimination in housing allocations.

16. An expanded public housing programme of new building and improvement is needed, particularly in the U.P.A.s, to ensure a substantial supply of good quality rented accommodation for all who need it, including single people. Each local authority's housing stock should include a range of types of accommodation, including direct access emergency accommodation.

17. The Housing (Homeless Persons) Act should be extended to cover all who are homeless. Homeless people should be offered a choice of accommodation.

18. There should be further moves towards the decentralisation of local authority housing services.

19. A major examination of the whole system of housing finance, including mortgage tax relief, is needed. It should have the objective of providing most help to those most in need.

20. The concept of 'care in the community' for people who might

otherwise be institutionalised must be supported by adequate resources to allow the provision of proper locally-based support services for people (especially women) caring for vulnerable and handicapped people.

21. Local authorities in boroughs which include U.P.A.s should, with other agencies, develop policies to establish and sustain community work with adequate resources.

22. The recommendations of the Lord Chancellor's Committee on the funding of Law Centres should be implemented immediately.

23. The Church, the Home Office and Chief Police Officers should give support to the work of Police Advisory Committees, and a Police Liaison Committee for Greater London should be established.

APPENDIX II
Trustees of the Fund

An up-to-date list of projects receiving support from the Fund may be obtained by writing to Church Urban Fund, Lambeth Place, London, SE1 7JU.

Index

projects, sponsors and principal characters